From Pain to Joy

God Has Already Worked It Out

Monica M Ambersley

Copyright © 2018 by Monica M Ambersley

From Pain to Joy – God Has Already Worked It Out!

All rights reserved. No part of this book may be reproduced, stored, duplicated in a retrieval system, or transmitted by any means, electronic, mechanical, photocopying, recording, or otherwise, without written permission from the copyright holder.

Limits of Liability and Disclaimer of Warranty: the author of this book have used their best efforts in preparing this material. The author makes no representation or warranties (expressed or implied), or merchantability for any particular purpose. The author shall in no event be held liable for any loss or other damages, including, but not limited to special, incidental, consequential, or other damages. The information presented in this publication is compiled from sources believed to be accurate, and the author assumes no responsibility for errors or omissions. The information in this publication is not intended to replace or substitute professional advice. The author specifically disclaims any liability, loss, or risk that is incurred as a consequence, directly or indirectly, of the use and application of any contents of this work.

Unless otherwise indicated, all Scripture quotations are taken from the Holy Bible, New International Version (NIV) © 1973, 1978, 1984, 2011 by Biblical, Inc and King James Version by the International Bible Society. Used by permission.

Scripture quotations marked NASB are from the New American Standard Bible, copyright © 1960, 1962, 1963, 1968, 1971, 1972, 1973, 1975, 1977, 1995. Used by permission.

First Published and Printed in the United Kingdom 2018

Published by Conscious Dreams Publishing

www.consciousdreamspublishing.com

Cover Design by Jacquelyn Jackson-Foster (Eden Creative Designs)

Editor: E. Lee Caleca

ISBN 978-1-912551-30-9

Dedication

I dedicate this entire book to the Holy Spirit who has been my Director, Counsellor and Guide. It has been an awesome experience and an exciting journey writing my first book. It has been a long time coming and has taken me twenty years to write. Because of His right timing, I owe it all to my Lord and Saviour, Jesus Christ!

My grandchildren, Imani-Marie and Cassius, my heart goes out to you both and to my four children, Leon, Melvin, Tiana and Ayeisha. I am excited about your future and your destiny as you grow into beautiful people.

To my future husband who God is preparing for me, I thank you for being obedient and trusting God. He has called you in a time such as this, and it is for His glory that He deserves our praises.

To all the young people who are struggling to fit into society, I pray that when you read this book you will find peace, joy and fulfilment in every area of your life. May you find joy through your pain, knowing that God has already worked it out for your good.

Acknowledgements

I must first acknowledge my Lord and Saviour Jesus Christ for giving me the privilege of expressing myself, candidly, and sharing my story. He has given me the gift to write on what God has done for me. I am grateful to God, not only for the completion of this book which has taken over twenty years to write, but for the lives that will be transformed by reading it.

To everyone whose books and articles I have read over the years and months, especially in 2017, may God richly bless you for encouraging me and others to step out from their comfort zone and step into their destiny.

Secondly, I would like to express my deepest and special gratitude to my writing coach, **Catherine E Storing**, my Writing Mama, for the many nights that we, the writing team, have stayed up through the small hours to write. I give the utmost praise to God, for allowing you to answer to the calling and to be used as an instrument to teach students to push out the book within us. Your obedience helped me and others to write and birthed out this book that will touch lives.

Thirdly, what can I say to this woman of God? **Pastor Kimberly Jones** (PK) you have been a pillar of strength to me. I thank you for your declarations over my life, through social media. You have encouraged me to step forward to my God-given calling.

Your *40 Days Declarations* inspired me to take up the challenge on Facebook Live and Periscope in 2016. As I began to 'speak those things' in faith for 40 days, I was able to see a transition that I have never experienced before. *Living by Purpose* is what I intend to do, in the name of Jesus! It has been a blessing and I thank God for you and your Ministry!

Fourthly, I would like to acknowledge **Bishop R C Blakes** for his word of encouragement on Periscope TV and Facebook Live where his words of encouragement have blessed me. I thank God for his Ministry and it has been a blessing listening to him teaching me and others the do's and don'ts of a relationship! You may not have been aware, but listening to your teachings and the powerful words in your book *'The Father Daughter Talk'* opened up many past hurt that remained locked up deep within me. After reading your book, I was able to embrace my healing and deliverance in which this book was then birthed.

To Danni Blechner and the Conscious Dreams Publishing team, a big thank you for all of you that were a part of the success of my book.

I extend a special thank you to my editor, Lee Caleca, who has done an amazing job. Also, thank you to Oksana Kosovan, my typesetter. We did it!

To my cover designer, Jacquelyn Jackson-Foster, for an excellent book cover design. Words cannot describe what this cover design mean to me. You are the best!

Lastly, I thank God for all the women of unshakeable faith who withstand and endure the storms of life but continue to remain firm and rooted in love. May your pain of the past be overthrown and replaced with joy, peace and happiness.

The Lens

The eyes of the Lens points to the direction of our hearts as it looks beneath the surface of what's in the inside of us.

The Lens focuses on destiny, new beginnings, new seasons penetrating the very soul of what is required from YOU to reach that goal.

The Lens sees fear, rejection, past hurt, brokenness and heartache. Can we achieve the hidden momentum of joy found through the Eyes of the Lens?

When life gets us down, sometimes it does, or we don't know what direction to take, the lens of our heart will direct us to where we ought to go, never taking its eyes off the destination at hand.

The surging waves that envelope each conscious decision is caught up in the turmoil of fear and confusion. But never in such a time as this, will we be far from the Lens that determine our destiny, goals and successes.

Our times are in His hands no matter how far we stray. For His eternal promise is rested on the soul of your heart, as your life become no more in pain, but a life of joy.

Foreword

If you have never observed the process someone goes through to transform their lives, then you are now in for a ride.

This book will take you on a journey from 'Pain to Joy'. It's a mission of looking for love from the places you thought you should find it and then having to let go because of disappointment and eventually finding that love in the arms of God. It's a story of strength, wisdom, and understanding. It's a story of a woman who has taken the time to reflect on her life and decides to extend the hand of forgiveness to those who had the responsibility of giving her unconditional love and support.

Monica's story is poignant in that we can all relate to various aspects of it. Her beautifully woven journey, reflected with Bible scriptures, highlights the different seasons of her life, and the promise of each verse demonstrates her spiritual growth and appreciation of how God was with her during each step.

Monica details the relationship she had with her mother and other family members in her formative years and the pain of rejection she experienced from them. This pain seeped into every area of her life which caused her to make life-changing decisions based on low self-esteem and an inability to trust people.

I can relate to her story as I too grew up in a first-generation Caribbean household. I had to watch my parents marry their Jamaican upbringing with the life and culture of the "motherland" England. The transition was difficult for them and for my siblings and me who were born into a crossfire of cultures.

Monica writes with an understanding of how and why her parents were unable to demonstrate their love for her and that they did the best that they could do based on their upbringing. I have personally come to realise that there are some things as adults we will never understand about our parents until we ourselves become parents. Then we can look back and appreciate the challenges and efforts our parents made.

Monica has taken the time to understand and appreciate that we cannot give what we do not have as parents and as people. Forgiveness is a key theme that runs through the book, and it will challenge the reader to examine their relationship with their own parents.

It's a transforming story of letting go of pain, pride, hurt and anxiety and embracing the true meaning of forgiveness. Transformation is something that we all desire to have and experience, but this process can come with pain.

Monica is a woman whose life started broken through personal pain and tragedy, who decided to rise from the ashes of her surroundings to become a woman who used these same ashes as a stepping stone to personal greatness and relevance.

Courage is something that is demonstrated daily by so many people in various situations. Some hide their courage and strength because they do not want to relive their story.

Monica Ambersley has chosen to share her story of rejection and how she moved from pain to joy. In retelling her painful journey, she demonstrates her strength and courage in coming out from under the devastation of rejection to become a woman who has decided to take the reins of her life and live as God intended her to. After reading her dramatic and compelling story, you will be challenged to start living your best life, and you will realise that what could have destroyed for evil, God can turn around and use for your good.

Monica's story reminds me of the Bible scripture that says that *"no weapon fashioned against you will prosper"* (Isaiah 54:17 ESV). As you read this story be prepared to cry a little and smile a lot at the excellent work God has done in Monica's life.

~ **Jenny Allen** ~
Life Coach – Heart of Refuge
London England

Contents

Acknowledgements v
The Lens vii
Foreword... ix
Introduction xv
    CHAPTER ONE. Rejection 19
    CHAPTER TWO. Forgive and Let Go.....................................43
    CHAPTER THREE. It is Only a Test.......................................51
    CHAPTER FOUR. In the Midst of Pain.................................55
    CHAPTER FIVE. Soul Ties...63
    CHAPTER SIX. Picking up the Pieces...................................69
    CHAPTER SEVEN. The Act of Forgiveness............................73
    CHAPTER EIGHT. Taking a Stand Against Fear...................83
    CHAPTER NINE. Hope for a Better Place 89
    CHAPTER TEN. Finding Joy Through the Pain...................97
    CHAPTER ELEVEN. Finding Peace 103
    CHAPTER TWELVE. Thinking Ahead 109
    CHAPTER THIRTEEN. Women of Unshakeable Faith 113
Conclusion 119
About the Author.. 125
References 127

Introduction

"I continue to believe that if children are given the necessary tools to succeed, they will succeed beyond their wildest dreams!"
~ David Vitter ~

As a teenager, I have always felt left out, unloved, hurt and betrayed. It does seem odd, I know! My time at home did not hold a happy memory, but a memory that, at times, caused me unhappiness. Most days there were good moments, but those moments would only last for a day or two.

My mother loved playing her guitar and, as she strummed the strings and began to sing, my siblings and I would start singing with her. The house would light up with the noise of tambourine and guitar as we sang our favourite choruses. As we huddled in one room with only one heater to warm the room, Mum would start playing her guitar, and it would indicate to me that she was in a good mood.

Most of my days while living at home were spent with my siblings, who were a little younger than myself, as we played the game of hide and seek around the house. Many of the games that we would play would find us dressing in up in our mother's high heel shoes, bag and fur coat.

Mum spent most of her days cleaning, ironing and cooking, while I found solace in reading. The aroma of soup would be on the cooker as we played in the garden. I looked forward to Saturdays because I would always know what was going to be for dinner. It was soup day!

Every Saturday, after my house chores were completed, I would go to the local library and sit for hours reading books until closing. In those days, libraries were quieter than they are now, and you would not see the rush of traffic of people and children entering the building. These were my solace moments where I could be me, away from the home and the rest of the siblings. I loved to read and as a 'bookworm', I would bury myself in the most exciting book that I could find in the library.

On Sundays, we would dress in our Sunday best for Church each week as we waited for the Church van to take us to Church. I looked forward to going to Church, as that was a good time to meet up with the other children who attended Sunday school each week.

At Church I was taught that God loves me, and He forgave my sins however small they were. I learnt that He would never cause me pain or hurt me. Love can speak volumes to a child when a parent reassures them that they are loved unconditionally.

My life experiences with rejection came at a point in my life when I was a young teenager. I wanted the love of my parents and also to feel a sense of belonging, something that I had not felt before at an early age. I am sure that they loved me as best they knew how, but it did not take away how I felt.

During the night, my parents would leave us to go to work. In those days, times were hard for Mum and Dad as they went to work to provide for my siblings and me. We were left each night to look after ourselves until they returned in the morning in time to see us to school. Because of the night shifts my mother had to work, I did not have the 'hugs' in the evening.

By the time I went to bed, she had already been in bed by six o'clock to start the night shift all over again and would ask us to wake her up for eight o'clock so she could go to work. I had often thought it would be nice if my mother could stay home with me instead of working nights.

Finding joy in the face of pain was difficult, and it came at a later time in my life where I struggled to fit in. My whole life had become disorientated, and it was only because of my belief and my trust in God that kept me sane over the years. I was able to find peace in the middle of my storm as I wrestled with life situations and calamities.

God's protection allowed me to experience His love more than ever before while I was in the most challenging time of my life, and His love has remained unconditionally throughout my entire life.

How many times have we looked within ourselves and found the cause of anguish and heartache that we may have experienced at one time in our lives?

There comes a time in one's life when we have to acknowledge where we have been and where we are now. As we often find ourselves struggling with pain emotionally, broken and unfortunate by the hidden emotion which has become embedded deep in past relationships, we often experience unworthiness, failure and rejection.

Self-esteem issues cloud our judgement and prevent us from being the best that we can be. Most of us, at some point in our lives, had moments where we had felt that nothing will change our situation. The light that shines to guide you in the dark moments will enable you to see past the hurt while you focus on the future and new beginnings. God is setting you up for greatness, and sometimes because of your emotions, you can miss the opportunity to receive. There have been moments where I have been in a place where things have become overwhelming.

It is my aim that the reader of this book will find comfort from it, knowing that the pain you face will eventually build you, so that you can proceed into your victory.

I pray that as you begin to read this book, you will identify the root cause of that damage and also experience the transition from pain to joy as it takes place. You may have experienced an overwhelming situation where you have carried with you for a long time, and it may not have been your fault! Perhaps it has never been your fault. You may have self-blamed, like myself, feeling guilty because of the abandonment you felt as a child or as an adult. But it will only be your fault if you don't find a way to forgive. When we step past those negative thoughts and forgive ourselves, we will begin to see things differently.

Our thoughts will be positive, giving us room to grow and bloom like a flower that opens its bud in the springtime. Too many times we run on empty not realising that our issues may have been passed on to our children. Nevertheless, every one of us will, at some point in our life, go through a season of pain. We all have to deal with pain, and it does not matter who you are or where you are in life. It is never too late to turn your life around the situation and do the impossible by faith. The pain you may be feeling right now will not define who you will be in the future!

It is a cry for help for many young people who will go undetected and lost in the system not knowing what direction to go. But I pray that God will do the impossible for every young person and women who are experiencing lack of self-worth and finding little value in themselves.

What is happening to you right now is happening for you; it is the process for your victory and your joy!

~ CHAPTER ONE ~

Rejection

YOU HAVE THE PERMISSION TO SPEAK WHAT MATTERS

"When you give yourself permission to communicate what matters to you in every situation you will have peace despite rejection or disapproval. Putting a voice to your soul helps you to let go of the negative energy of fear and regret."

~ **Shannon L. Alder** ~

Rejection has been a part of my life as far back as I can remember, and it has been an experience that I would never want to encounter again. It has caused me pain in the past and has caused heartache in my relationships with other people.

For many of us who have felt the sting of rejection and painful situations, there are wounds that remain embedded deep in our thoughts, and these wounds have caused us to act out in desperation and fear. We have all gone through some level of rejection and it does not necessarily come from parents, but may also come from relationships, family and friends. When we feel rejected, we remain stuck in those moments and unable to move forward. These deep-rooted issues affect our perceptions, feelings and emotions and, consequently, the way we interact with others. We may find ourselves living in a state of confusion as we grapple to find the right solution to our pain.

Holding on to that pain will send us to another dimension of mistrust, self-denial, resentment, and bitterness. Unresolved issues that remain as a 'friend' in our adult life will never allow us to find a place of peace and reconciliation. And inevitably, there will be a time when those pangs of pain will seep through into our relationships with others.

Sometimes it can affect you both spiritually and physically; not giving you the opportunity to let go and live. It can cause you to relive the event of those past hurts over and over again in your mind, which can produce added stress and emotions, further skewing your perception of your life and the people in it.

Children who experience long-lasting rejection over a period, as they struggle to find their identity in society, become children who are receptive to rejection. Sometimes children or young people will give up on the ability to develop on their current situation by not sustaining a relationship with children of their age. We often see children's behaviour increase rapidly, in a negative way, which can lead to shyness, lack of self-confidence, low self-esteem, chronic self-doubt, depression, social anxiety, and timid behavioural pattern.[1]

Unfortunately, I was one of those children who was shy and timid, but always the one that had to take the blame for everyone's missteps. If our house fell down, I would be the one that would be blamed for letting it happen! That was how it was at home. It was that bad! I am probably over exaggerating a bit. But on a serious note, it was frightening at times, that someone should be blamed for everything!

My father was not always at home and Mum was 'left' to look after myself and the five siblings on her own, until my father decided that he had a home to come back to. Although he was not around as much as he should have been, as he was always working or socialising with friends, he was very different from my mother. He would often play football with us or take us to the park to run. We were young and he would always win the race before we even got to the finish line! I think it was one of a few happy moments that I shared with him. Those happy moments in a child's life are the most precious thing that they can remember, spending time with parents who love and care for them.

My father was not a very educated person, but he knew how to draw. He only needed to look at a picture and sketch it skilfully. In his free time when he was not working, he would often teach me how to write my name and my date of birth at the age of five. Spelling was my favourite! He would tell me to write the answer on his Pools paper which he used when betting on the horses. There was something special about writing our answers on the Pools result sheet. By the time I went to school, I was always 'tops' in the class with my spelling.

My dad was tall and handsome and had a great sense of humour which showed in his laughter. He was laid back and nothing seem to bother him. I can honestly tell you I look like my dad, a resemblance that was strong amongst my siblings. I had inherited his bone structure which I carried well into my adult life. I can remember not loving that bone structure on my face, but now I embrace it with pride. Well sort of, as I often wonder if the resemblance to my father was my downfall!

Have you ever felt rejected by one person or another?

So often we have rejected God and denied Him, but when we read 1 Peter 2:4, it metaphorically explains to us that the *"living stone who was rejected by men but chosen and precious"* did not reject us. It does not matter what others have said about you or have hurt you in the past. You are chosen to be the best that you can be.

> *"As you come to Him, a living Stone rejected by men, but in the sight of God, chosen and precious"*
> **(1 Peter 2:4)**

We may not feel special right now, but despite what is going on in your life or what anyone wants to say about you, God loves you, and He will never reject you. God said it, and there is nothing anyone can say about it. God's word is final, He has the last word, and His word does not come back as a lie. We are more than conquerors to those who are overcomers.

> *"What, then, shall we say in response to these things? If God is for us, who can be against us?"*
> **(Romans 8:31)**

Define Who You Are

In my experience, during my childhood, the love of a mother, who felt emotionally disconnected from me, made me feel worthless and inadequate. I believe my mother loved me as best as she could. Although she was always around caring for her family, she did not allow the time to spend time with me. I am not saying that my mother did not care for me, but the love she was supposed to give me as a child was absent. For a long time, as much I could remember, I had always felt that she did not love me as much as my other siblings. But over the years I was able to forgive my mother and begin a relationship with her in the years after.

Despite what I went through in those critical years of my life, I began to redefine who I was. I was not the person that became 'messed' up, but I became who God wanted me to be, a woman of valour.

On my sixteenth birthday, while living at home, my future looked bright; I began a makeup line. Yes, a makeup line all on my own. Can you believe it! I started selling makeup products and had a list of clients, including my family! So, yes, my future looked bright from my end! Everything seemed ready to set off, and as I saw beyond my years, I could almost smell success! A makeup line will be the next move I once thought, or perhaps I can take up modelling! Many people had once told me that I had the face of a model, slim and slender with prominent bone structure.

I was becoming an entrepreneur in my own right, selling my own line of cosmetics and practicing how to apply them. Once a week, I would take the time to travel on the train to collect my supplies. I was enjoying the freedom to do 'my thing', and the idea of selling my products was exciting. It was my way of showing myself that I can make it as an entrepreneur when no one believed in me. I was determined to make something of myself. I was defining who I was, and it felt good!

As parents, it is crucial for us to invest in our children's future, so that they may receive the right start in life. It does not have to be through monetary gifts, but the push and reassurance can encourage your child to reach for more than they have and be the best that they can.

At the age of seventeen, four weeks before my eighteen birthday, my life made an enormous turn that nearly destroyed me, emotionally. I was involuntarily forced to do something out of my will; I was asked to leave my home with nothing but a twenty-pound note in my purse.

Where was I going? How was I going to survive? I had to face this big world on my own at a young age. I loved my mother dearly, and deep down she may not have meant to act on her emotions and not knowing what the consequences of her action would do to me. In years that followed, I now know that over the years she has regretted the decision that she made. There were questions that I had asked myself as I fought back the tears while experiencing fear for the first time. It became tough for me to digest all this in one breath, let alone swallow it. My mum, who I have always loved, had rejected me despite how young I was. Her decision left me vulnerable; a minor on the streets of London.

It happened one bright afternoon, as I recollected the event of the day. I was not happy at home and, because I always felt picked on by my other siblings, I stayed at a friend's home that night. It was not my intention to stay out, but the buses had stopped running and I decided to stay until the morning. The following morning, I made the long journey back to my home and apologised for not coming home that night. I was not sure if my mother realised I was not home, but as I spoke to her she did not show any interest. As I went upstairs to the bedroom, I shared with my older sister, I could see that my mum was on edge and that something was brewing in the atmosphere. What happened that afternoon changed my life forever!

Downstairs, my mother was cooking and cleaning the house and I heard her muttering to herself in the kitchen. At the bottom of the stairs she asked me to do something for her, but for some reason I did not hear what she was saying.

Between not knowing what she had asked me and not obeying her instruction, it became a blur to me. It was in that instant that she said if I continued to 'answer her back' she would call the police. As teenagers, we laughed when my mum said she was calling the police for answering her back as we just thought it was an empty threat. You know those 'answer back moments' when you said something or another under your breath to avoid a showdown? We did not take her seriously when she said that. Why should we? But we laughed not believing that she was serious, after all, we were only teenagers! The words *'Go on, then!'* were the last words that my mother heard down the stairs and they enraged her. My sister had told her to 'go on then' leaving me victim to those words. These words that would alter my life forever.

The words *'Go on then,'* caused a life-changing avenue or chapter in my life to begin. Again, I was blamed for someone else's comment at my expense.

Mum had come to the UK in the 60s from the Caribbean, leaving behind my older brother in Jamaica, to live with my dad who she later married. It was hard for her to bring up six children with my dad and she found it difficult at times. Mum had left behind her family in the Caribbean to live in the UK, a place that made her feel alienated and alone. So, I can understand the frustration of doing things on her own and not see the opportunity to connect with her children individually. In my mother's frustration, she would often use words to me, *'One rotten sheep can spoil the flock!'* Yes, I said it! I was a rotten sheep, I thought, that was spoiling the family, and it was there I felt not wanted! Those negative name tags became my clothing that destroyed my self-esteem!

After which seemed like hours, the police arrived, and a loud knock at the front door would be heard across the house as my mother opened the front door to let them in. There they were, outside my bedroom in their suit of blue with their helmet on! Outside the bedroom I shared with my older sister, the police stood almost patiently not knowing what to ask me. I am not sure if they knew the reason they had been 'summoned' to our house.

How on earth can this be happening? I live in the United Kingdom where there are laws for underage minors and here were these two policemen waiting to ask me to leave without asking me what the issue was.

No, I was not pregnant, and I was not involved in anything criminal!

I wanted to scream and scream, but no words came out as I stared in disbelief and shock. As I stood in my nightdress at the bedroom door, I asked them why they were here. I was petrified, and my heart was thumping out of my chest as I stood naively staring at the policemen. In my disbelief, I remembered saying to them, 'Why do I have to leave?' and their reply was, 'Your mother has asked us that you leave the house, and we cannot leave until you leave with us.' The policeman's words now added more salt to the hurt as he spoke to me trying to make me understand.

Should I refuse to go? Or be rebellious and disobey my Mum over these two strangers? But no, I went as a sheep to the 'slaughter' to the unknown. Growing up in the early 70s, we were taught to obey our parents and honour them with respect. I did not know what the consequences would be if I refused to go.

What?! I stood looking at them in disbelief. My sister's decision to 'dare' my mum had become a sick joke I could not comprehend. While all this was going on, my sister said nothing to stop them from allowing me to leave the house.

What Was the Issue Here?

As I gathered up enough clothes I could carry to no man's land, tears began to roll down my face like a tsunami flood.

How many teenagers have felt like this? How many of us have become adults and find ourselves going through the traumas of rejection and hurt that we have long forgotten? We often dress up the rejection and the pain with beautiful clothes and makeup to hide the pain we are enduring. Sometimes we are reluctant to let our loved ones know we are hurting. According to the Children Society: *"Parents and other adult carers have a responsibility to ensure the safety and welfare of children and young people under the age of eighteen, yet research has shown that many young people (primarily teenagers) are forced to leave home."* [2]

Here I was, standing outside the family home, which was home for the last fourteen years; stranded on the street with no place to go. The police officers had done what they were called to do, and they left almost immediately as the front door shut behind me. They had made sure I was out of the house before they were satisfied before driving away. It is ironic that two law enforcing officers, who I know should be protecting a youngster or a minor, drove off into the sunset without a backward glance.

It was from that point of my experience that day, with rejection and hurt, I felt the sense of hopelessness and despair. I was optimistic for my future, that now looked like my dismal future. I cannot remember how long I stood outside, but by then the police officers were well gone.

I had already made up my mind that I was not going to return to the place where I felt abandoned and hurt. Why should I?

Like a young bird who was thrown out of its nest and finding no way to get back in, I made my way to 'nowhere' land; not knowing what was to become of me. In reality, my days of the nest were over, never to return, although it became hard for me to digest this in one bite, the painful reality was real! Because of those three words, *'Go on, then'*, my life made an enormous turn that changed the way I saw things.

Barely knowing what to do or where to live, I was unfamiliar with the outside world because of my sheltered life. It had always been school, church and home. I never had the opportunity to know anything else; I was not allowed to go anywhere. I did not even know how to be sociable nor was I streetwise, let alone able to live on my own. My life as far as I can remember has always been sheltered!

In those days we were not allowed to go out as children and meet up with friends of our age and explore our surroundings while growing up. The outside world was foreign to me, but here I was, the little abandoned skinny-legged teenager, stranded outside with what little clothing I could gather.

The Bible states in Luke 10:16, *"Jesus said, he who rejects you, rejects Me."*

We can look more in-depth at the causes and results of rejection in young people where rebellion is spurned by rejection and hurt emotions. Almost everyone will, at one point in their lives, experience rejection starting in their childhood. And even if it's only in their own perception, it doesn't hurt any less. It is at this point that the devil will use the fear of rejection to avert us from taking steps to reach our destiny. Although it seems that we take on the energy of rejection, avoiding it as best as we can, we miss the chance to build stable and loving relationships as we protect ourselves from the side effects of rejection.

We all go through the emotions of loneliness when we are isolated from loved ones or those close to us. Loneliness plays a critical role in the life of a teenager who is left abandoned, which can be a dramatic and a painful experience. In time, these feelings have an impact on the body, mind and soul. God does not reject us, nor does He forsake us, although many times we have rejected Him to live a life without Him.

My rejection caused me to turn my back on God because I could not believe that He had allowed this to happen. I felt, also, that the Church had let me down as a teenager and that they did not have my best interest at heart. While rejection can be life-changing, the Word has promised you that rejection is from the world and not from God.

There was no one else I could turn to in my time of despair, not even ChildLine if that had been available. ChildLine was not available for me when I was a teenager, and having no one to turn to for help, left me isolated and alone.

Parents who are born in an unsupportive family, having children of their own, will find it difficult to nurture their children. But for many, the opportunity to receive the encouragement or to have a mother to hug them, reassuring them that everything will be okay, may never come. And because they have experienced these negative emotions, their ability to show love to their children will be absent. While parents may learn in the future, through their own experience from their parents, they inevitably live what they have learned. In their ability to be good parents, the skills to care and love their children would often be 'styled' out in their own parenting transferring the same pain to their children.

Can a Parent Teach What They Do Not Know?

Because the Church was not supportive, which left me vulnerable as a teenager, I became prey to their judgemental words, which negatively affected me. One of the reasons many teenagers or adolescents leave Church comes from the root of 'church wounds' they experienced as a young person. Rejected because they did something that the Church deemed 'wrong' in their eyes. The 'backbench' policy that made them feel rejected and isolated; instead of protecting them and giving them a safe haven where they could find refuge, it caused many to feel hurt and ashamed.

I know God loved me, but at the time I could not understand why I was the only one that had to endure what I went through. I am sure many teenagers can relate to my situation and now, in this era, many are still ashamed to talk about it. Sometimes past issues and bad experiences are the reason we are the person we are today. Although the past is put in place to teach and mould us in the way God has planned for us; we learn from our past failures only by allowing ourselves to be vulnerable.

As I walked down the street with no direction, my mind began to race, not knowing what was going to happen to me. 'Where am I going?'

'What direction shall I take and what now?' No answer, but the silent rain that bounced off the ground like large teardrops, that became my tears!

As 'I think of God, and I moaned, overwhelmed with longing for His help…' (**Psalm 77:3**). 'Why have You rejected me so long? (**Psalm 74:1**). '…do not let me sink any deeper' (**Psalm 69:14**). 'I am exhausted from crying for help; my throat is parched. My eyes are swollen with weeping, waiting for my God to help me. Those who hate me without a cause outnumber the hairs on my head' (**Psalm 69:2-4**). 'I cry to You for help when my heart is overwhelmed' (**Psalm 61:2**). 'Fear and trembling overwhelm me, and I cannot stop shaking' (**Psalm 55:4**). 'Why am I so discouraged? Why is my heart so sad?' (**Psalm 42:5**).

I began wondering where on earth I was going and what direction I should take. But as my mind raced full speed, God was looking after me. I remembered as I walked, not knowing the direction I was taking, a family friend who came to mind who lived a mile away, took me into her home and sheltered me for a while.

God works mysteriously behind the scene, and He is always there when we think He isn't there. There are times when we do not understand how God works things out for our good, but His timing is always the right timing.

God the Protector

Living on my own was new to me, primarily as a young teenager living away from home. I was not accustomed to living apart from my family, and it was hard for me to adjust. The feeling was strange not being in the same household where I lived as a child with my siblings. It was in my loneliness I became aware and soon discovered that no one came looking for me. Following the weeks and months, I waited for my parents to come and take me home. No one came. There were no mobile phones or WhatsApp for them to message me, but they knew where I was; ten minutes away from home. Sadly, I had no choice but to adjust to my 'new life' on my own.

Countless of parents struggle with past issues that they continue to afflict on the lives of their children, sometimes unknowingly. Many have not found the help needed so they can relate to their children adequately. The painful past they may have experienced themselves are later passed on to their children in words and actions. The effect of words that destroy self-awareness instead of building up confidence, self-esteem, self-worth and values as well as the name tags that are placed on their children, never considering that those names would be acted out in the future as they approach the adolescent years and often in the mature years. Although I was blessed to have two parents, the fact remains they were supposed to love me and nurture me.

As days, nights turned into years; no one enquired after me; I became a distant memory in the life of my family; ostracised for what seemed like an eternity.

I had so many dreams to look forward to and things I wanted to accomplish, but two people who did not think about the possibilities of what they were doing damaged me emotionally. Temporarily.

The dreams I once had were far away in the distance as I struggled with a life situation for which I had no or little experience. Although life goes on whether we choose to move on or stay behind, finding the courage to dust off and keep it moving is the only way forward, despite the heartache, and the misfortunes that we experience.

People will come into our lives, and we may lose some along the way; our circle of friends will change. But there is a season where we will see growth, a season to uproot, a season to weep, and a season to be at peace.

Along the way, we will learn real-life skills which will teach us how to remain strong, how to love ourselves and how to know who we are. We can be the best of who we are! It's wise to grasp this methodology because life will continue whether we choose to move on or stay behind.

The year 1979 was a year when racism was at its peak and, as youngsters, we were vigilant on the streets, afraid of being attacked or racially abused. Here I was, on the streets with no parental covering. These were the people I felt had the power to love me, care for me and nurture me while I was young and innocent.

Teenagers and young people today are accustomed to having all kinds of freedoms, but I had no experience outside of my family home, being brought up in a Christian background all my life. As far as I can remember, we were taught to obey our parents according to the Bible teachings. So, when I found myself in a place outside of my comfort zone, a place that was alien to me, I was shattered and broken.

My growing up in Church and attending Sunday school was the only thing that I can remember that may have saved my life. While living outside of my parents' home, the seeds had already been planted by the years attending Sunday school and learning about who God was. Sunday school worked out well for me, not only as a teenager but as an adult. It was there I learnt about the love of God and His love for me. I was able to depend on God for His guidance and protection throughout my life. Although the sense of belonging was present, I was able to look past my hurt and see something new.

Moving Forward

I told myself, a child is a blessing, and because a child is a blessing, a baby will bring me joy. To me, it was a blessing to have a child since I was feeling unloved and abandoned. It may not have been a good idea since

I had not dealt with my rejection. It was the only thing that I thought would fill the void in my life.

Isolated and ostracised from my family and left abandoned, I tried to cope with unresolved issues from my painful past. The past events of the years were prohibiting me from seeing any joy.

> *"Can a woman forget her nursing child and have no compassion on the son of her womb? Even these may forget, but I will not forget you. Behold, I have inscribed you on the palms of my hands...'*
> **(Isaiah 49:15-16 NASB)**

My temporary living space saw me looking for somewhere to sleep and renting a room was not an option; I had no money. There was nowhere for me to go, and I was afraid and alone, not knowing where I was going to find a place to live. There I met 'Him' who was four years older than I was. I told 'Him' about my dilemma and that I was not living at home. We became friends and he offered me a place to stay for a while.

Many teenagers who go through the motion of rejection, will experience the same emotions I once felt, which can see them becoming pregnant at an early age because of the lack of love that they did not receive at home.

According to Amelia Hill of The Guardian, *"the rate of teenage pregnancy in the UK has decreased in the last twenty years since 1960. The Office for National Statistics has given details of the fall in the rate of teenage pregnancy from age fifteen to nineteen. Although there are some who tend to fall outside the statistics, a few teenage girls who are lacking parental love sadly are drawn to find it outside of their home."* [3]

Although we try to cover up our pain of rejection, the Bible states in:

"Take heed, do not turn to iniquity, for you have chosen this rather than affliction."

(Job 36:21)

In 1982, my first child, a son, was born, and he was the most adorable baby that I could have imagined. As I fondly remember the joy I felt as I held the tiny bundle in my arms, I could not believe that I could now feel love and affection for such a small human being. I remembered feeling that I was now at a place in my life to love and be loved back. I loved my baby, and I was the happiest person on earth! Although he was a joy to me and the love of my life, the void in my life, the messed-up hurt, had not disappeared and it reared its ugly head in my life again.

The pain I experienced began hovering over in the background of my life reminding me of my past rejection and abandonment. The isolation and loneliness and the pain of rejection once again became my present companion as I suffered a new crisis in the years that followed.

As the years went by it became unbearable, and I would sometimes take refuge in my thought life by asking God to help me, to give me the strength to move on. I needed help desperately, but there was no one I could speak to about how I was feeling. I struggled with low self-esteem issues, and my lack of confidence created a barrier to pursuing my dreams and goals. I had so much that I wanted to do with my life, but there was no encouragement or motivation to drive me or to push me to my destiny. My dreams and vision looked bleak and dismal; I was viewing them from a distance, and no amount of tears can ever make you comprehend how I felt at that moment.

Many women build their lives around their husbands or children, where they can continue to exhibit the damage and the effects of the impact that rejection can cause. Coming to terms with rejection is one thing but dealing with the problem is another. Rejection can also come from the womb as a seed, but often it is nurtured in the years as the seed begins to grow. It can come from words that were said over your life, spoken or unspoken. As parents, it is crucial that we talk to other teenagers or a young person who may be going through serious situations. Talking to them and showing them that you care is the first step to understanding them. Although some may not want to talk to anyone about the problems they are facing, showing them that someone has their back, is a blessing for them. First, they need to know that you can be trusted, and that the conversation is confidential; unless they are a cause for alarm where they may need professional advice. Secondly, it is important that they are understood and not judged.

When we go through this process of resolving our feelings of being unloved, we should use the experience to elevate ourselves and others to greatness. As women, we have the opportunity to excel from where we are despite our past hurt!

Although looking back over the years and potential careers that I should have had, I realise it was only temporary, as I remain positive. God was already on the job, and He was working it out for me in the background. When we are in our state of mess, God is tenderly looking after our interest and working it out for our good. He is a good God!

During the process that I went through, I would later forgive my mother. It was not easy but, because I wanted to move forward with my life, I decided to let go of the situation and embrace my healing with open arms. What was the use of me holding onto grudges and hurt that had once left me in a trail of despair and anger?

Over the years, I began putting together the pieces which had left me numb with hurt. Years of rejection in my relationship with my mother began to take control of my life. Everything that I thought about myself was of a pessimistic nature. I had no value in myself, and I suffered from low-esteem that made me look pitiful to the eyes of others.

I wore makeup to cover up the hurt, emptiness and the rejection because it was the only way possible to mask the damaged emotion. My makeup helped me to mask the internal wound, and by default, it was my way of showing people that I was now getting on with my life. I became a chronic shopaholic covering every disappointment and hurt with new clothes and shoes. Buying clothes was the only way that would make me feel loved; loving myself was the only solution that I knew worked.

My years of trying to fit into society, trying to belong and having no one to understand what I was going through did not allow me to meet new people in my younger self; I trusted no one. The years of rejection in my relationships began to take its toll in the way I saw my life.

After the birth of my eldest son, I was again blessed some years later, with three more wonderful children. As my life began to move forward in a positive way, I realised that the traumas of my childhood had affected me as a mother. I did not want my children to go through what I did so instead I showered them with gifts and presents that fed off of my own insecurities. Without realising that I was wrapping them up in 'cotton wool' I was building a security blanket for them. I tried not to let them go out on their own, which caused them to be vulnerable because they were not experiencing anything, gaining life skills or learning how to navigate their small world and use their judgement. It was frightful to see, and the more I felt the rejection and insecurities, the more I left my children frustrated by it. I love my children, who are my life, but I was determined not to let them to go through the pitfalls that I once had to endure as a teenager.

The years of trying to fit in and be accepted in the family became a struggle which I found burdensome. But in hindsight, I may not have done the things that I am doing now if the circumstances were different. It was through my pain and rejection that prompted me, after all those years, to write this book. One of my desires was to start my life positively and forget the past.

When we fail to look inside ourselves and find the reason why certain things happen to us, we can see ourselves remaining in the same position feeling bitter and resentful. We can experience rejection, at some time or other, in any area of our life regardless of maturity or status. Rejection does not exempt anyone from experiencing it, and it may attack you when you are most vulnerable. It is an emotional spiral that can remain with you for the rest of your life if it is not dealt with quickly.

Dealing with rejection is the first step to your spiritual healing. When you go through brokenness and pain, you can often succumb to the feeling of guilt. Rejection can tell you that it is your fault when things do not go the right direction. Rejection does not care who you are, nor the positions that you may hold. Rejection will never be your friend, but a soul destroyer, marriage breaker and a relationship dismantler.

There are many elements for rejection which may present themselves through many factors:

1. Families
2. Friends
3. Soul-Ties
4. Marriages
5. Church Wounds
6. Ungodly Relationships

Many of these areas can have a significant impact on our lives and can be devastating when we are at our weakest. However, God is saying,

"Behold I come quickly; and My reward is with Me, to give every man according to his work shall be."

(Revelation 22:12)

So, regardless how small or significant, critical, short-term or long-term, rejection will only have the power to take over if you allow it to control your lives. Feeling helpless in the face of a crisis can also leave you feeling paralysed spiritually.

We often see many young people suffering from rejection in the Church, too afraid to speak to someone of the struggles that they face, because of the fear of judgemental remarks or finger-pointing.

When young people 'act up', as parents we should ensure that we find the time to see what their current situation is and what is happening in their life. There are underlining issues that can force a child or a young person to react in certain situations. Because rejection can come to us through different conditions and circumstances, the key to combat rejection is first to love yourself and rebuild your self-esteem. The key is to forgive those who have wronged or hurt you, wilfully or unknowingly, are the first steps to recovery. Forgiving ourselves of past mistakes and bad choices can relieve us mentally and spiritually giving us freedom of the mind.

Family Relationships – Did you feel rejection through your parents?

_____
_____
_____
_____
_____
_____
_____
_____
_____
_____

How are you coping with rejection?

_____
_____
_____
_____
_____
_____
_____
_____
_____
_____

We can experience intimidation and mistreatment, physically and emotionally, by the words that are said to us. A mother's wound can be another cause for rejection which can manifest itself in the spiritual realm.

Below there are ten reasons why you need to eliminate rejection from your life:

1. **Forgive yourself** for the mistakes or bad decisions; it was not your fault that things did not work out.
2. **Know who you** are and what your values are.
3. **Be true to yourself**; you are unique; and there is only one of you.
4. You are irreplaceable.
5. Do not blame yourself. It is not your fault.
6. **Remain positive** and focused.
7. Know that **God loves you** unconditionally.
8. **Forgive** the perpetrator and move on.
9. Love yourself.
10. **Believe** in yourself.

We have the power to move a mountain, by faith, and to move forward to receive our God-given life!

Write down how you value yourself. What criteria do you use to consider someone valuable?

~ CHAPTER TWO ~

Forgive and Let Go

EVERY ENCOURAGEMENT IS A STEP FORWARD

"I am not discouraged, because every wrong attempt discarded is another step forward."

~ Thomas Edison ~

When our father and mother abandon or give up on you, the Lord will adopt us! How powerful is that! God will never leave us because He loves us so much and His undying love has depicted this to us. The love that He has shown to us is stronger than those that are close to us.

"When my father and mother forsake me, the Lord will take me up"
(Psalms 27:1)

For that reason, God's love does not change nor, does it cause us to feel rejected and ashamed. Our heavenly Father loves us so much He sacrificed His Son, Jesus Christ, to die on a Cross for us.

> *"We have been crucified with Christ. It is no longer us who live, but Christ who lives in us. And the life we now live in the flesh we live by faith in the Son of God who loved us and gave Himself for us"*
> **(Galatians 2:20)**

Letting go of past hurts will empower us to live a better life, free from the past and free from the power of negative feelings of emotions. The longer we spend undeveloped or unmovable in our personal or spiritual growth, the more we leave things to chance, only to find ourselves stuck in the same situation year after year. Sometimes when we are feeling emotionally drained, we should **step back** and assess what is really happening. We often let our emotions override positive thinking without questioning how we are feeling. However, everything does not have to remain the same regardless where we are in life, and we do not have to be consumed by our emotions. When we go through certain situations and rediscover our purpose through the pride, anger and hurt, we often find that what has happened to us was meant for our tenacious goals, which in turns strengthen us. We can sometimes learn that our past issues, which seemed difficult to comprehend, was intended for our good. Things may not feel right at this moment, but in time as you read and equip yourself in the Word, your pain will empower you to grow spiritually.

Maybe you are struggling right now, as you try to keep your head above 'water', but the moment that you look at things a little clearer, the change from the negative mindset will change your circumstance and the way you feel about yourself. For a change to happen, **first**, you will have to **learn to forgive** and let go of past hurts, anger and pride. By holding on to unforgiveness, bitterness and pride, you will find that these obstacles may prevent you from raising the bar on your future.

Secondly, forgive the person who has done you wrong. Don't be too hard on yourself. We sometimes blame ourselves for someone else's wrongdoing which can leave us feeling guilty and deflated. One thing we always have to remember that forgiveness is not for the other person, but for you! Forgiveness makes room for **you** to embrace your God-given life without the baggage of guilt and condemnation. What we have heard over the years was the wrong perception of what is forgiveness, and because of the deception and lies that the enemy has told many of us, we believed it and refused to forgive others.

As I reflected on my life, my desire to forgive others and myself for the wrong decisions and choices that I have made, I knew that my mindset, and how I saw myself, was changing. My outlook on life was becoming perceivable as I began to work on myself. Eventually, I was able to let go and forgive my mother for the wrong choices she made over my life and forgiving myself for the lost years I spent blaming myself for failed opportunities. When we take full responsibility for the failed opportunities that we have lost, we will find that we can soar like an eagle without its wing clipped. In reality, when an eagle has its wings cut, it will have limits to where it can go; unable to move freely. Does that sound familiar?

> *"Eagles fly alone at a high altitude and not with sparrows nor do they mix with other smaller birds."* [4]

Fear of forgiving can also lead to rejection and pride, and often it becomes difficult to forgive others. What we are saying, when we don't forgive, we do not want to exonerate others of any wrongdoings, because they are not qualified for our forgiveness. However, you have to be willing to forgive, not for the other person, but for you to let go and move forward. But if you hold on to pride, which can be your major setback, it may become hard for you to forgive others and yourself.

Today, find ways where you can forgive someone for the wrongs that they have done to you. It is never too late to forgive others. Sometimes you need to forgive them so that your conscience and outlook on life remain positive. We must all strive to forgive others because our faults are not measured by what has happened to us, but the ability to set standards that align us with the Word of God.

Re-living the past in my mind was not the way that God intended me to live my life, but for me to live it in perfect peace was to let go and live, love and receive joy! Everything that I once knew or understood, in my younger self, was a lie. A lie that told me my past was hindering my purpose and my destiny. Satan, the Father of all lies, will not stop until he destroys every plan that God has for you. He intends to eradicate your future, your destiny and your hope.

We often find ourselves in this predicament when we think that we have no achievements to show and for a while it limits our progress. However, the biggest achievement we can gain is letting go and refuse to be controlled by our past. There are many people who find themselves going down the same spiral of destruction, even after twenty years, because they refuse to let go of past hurts.

Putting God first in my life was the best thing that I could have done and it could not have come at a better time. As God so lovingly poured His love in me, a new awakening was about to happen that would change my life forever. God was about to do something new, and there was nothing anyone could do to stop it. My season to let go of past issues, that corroded my life, was now beginning to take place. God's plan was to transform and use me to His will as He touched my life and the lives of others, when no one has ever made a difference. His arm that lovingly embraced me was warm and inviting as He promised me, in His Word, that He will never leave me nor forsake me.

It was through the pain I felt all those years, I was able to see things for what they were. My understanding of who God is was now becoming conspicuous and transparent from the God that my mother knew. I learnt that He was a God that loves me, and that He was not angry with me, despite my shortcomings. He loved me before conception and He would not cast me out into the sea of forgetfulness because He had always covered me when I was not aware of it.

In every aspect of my entire life, as far as I could remember, God has always covered me inside and outside, in many areas of my life that were unreachable to me.

I guess I can ask this question, a genuine question: *'Why did I not see this before?'* Our emotions can cloud our judgement by telling us that we are useless and unworthy, and without using our feelings that create wrong choices that are detrimental to our destiny!

God waits patiently for our change before He reveals to us why He allowed certain things to happen to us for our growth. The pain of hurt I felt all those years was a process I had to go through to let me become the person I am now.

You too can be the person that God has called you to be, and no one can know what this is except God. He has made you in His own image so you can rise up from where you are and soar like an eagle.

God's plan for our lives may not be one that we understand or appreciate. His plans for us is to protect us from every distraction and obstacle that we face. We have to believe, and trust that God will deliver us from strongholds that may come to hinder our progress.

What are strongholds?

Strongholds are spiritual battles that we may face in our daily lives. There are spiritual battles that we may continue to fight as we read the Word of God.

> *"For though we walk in the flesh, we do not war after the flesh: For the weapons of our warfare are not carnal but mighty through God to the pulling down of strongholds"*
>
> **(2 Corinthian 10:3-4)**

The Bible states that He knows the plans that He has for every one of us and that every evil that Satan has planned for us, God has worked it out for us. !

> *"For I know the plans I have for you," declares the Lord, "plans to prosper you and not to harm you, plans to give you hope and a future."*
>
> **(Jeremiah 29:11)**

'Let go and live' is one of the themes that has empowered me to forgive and let go of all the things that have hurt me. Through the most challenging time of my life I was able to forgive others for the wrong they did to me by moving forward with my life. Because of everything that has happened to me, the enemy was determined to destroy me spiritually, but God's plan was not for me to be destroyed but for me to raise my standard high. When we are not in control of our lives, God is in control. At times when Satan thought he was winning; God continued to be in control; undefeated!

There is power in forgiveness. Forgiveness can release you from the feeling of guilt and bitterness. Holding on to unforgiveness may leave you torn and battered when you do not forgive. Holding on to past issues will affect how you interact with others.

All our relationships can be affected by our current situation or problems and the baggage we carry around with us, and we can find ourselves blaming others of our misadventures. Learning to effectively deal with all our issues is the only way to maintain healthy relationships. In the same way you want to be forgiven for your missteps, you should show forgiveness to anyone who hurts you. Sometimes it is unintentional. **Talk things out**. Not every hurt was meant to be so.

As we get older, we may come to realise that we have to take responsibility for our own actions and decisions. This is what determines our spiritual growth. Although it may be painful to face, many of the rejections we perceived were borne from our parents' issues they had experienced, and which have continued to cause pain. Because I was 'trained' in rejection, many of the relationships I encountered in later life may not have been rejections at all, but only what I perceived as rejection because my self-esteem was so low. I had no skill in knowing how a real honest relationship should be formed, whether it was with friends, acquaintances, business or anything else.

At an early age, it was miserable to know that during those years I felt I was just an existence; I was only there! Finding joy in the face of pain was hard. I was alone and afraid, and it was only my belief in God that kept me over the years. There is one thing that I will hold on to, that God is a God of second chances. He is bigger than our problems and much bigger than our situations.

If you are experiencing emotional pain and you are not sure if you will ever see a light in the tunnel, I am here to remind you that God is able. If He has done it for me, He can also do the same for you.

Sometimes we can feel 'stuck' in our circumstances and face the difficulty of submitting to the blame that we hold onto. But as we allow ourselves and believe that we are not the victim and **stop** blaming someone else for our misadventure, we will find that we can move forward and embrace our future with confidence. And **when you forgive others, your forgiveness will lead you to love others**.

Is there a particular issue that you would like to let go of? And why?

_____
_____
_____
_____
_____
_____

What is preventing you from letting go?

_____
_____
_____
_____
_____
_____
_____

Write down the things that you have not let go of, and why?

_____
_____
_____
_____
_____
_____
_____

~ CHAPTER THREE ~

It is Only a Test

LOOKING AT PAIN THROUGH A LOOKING GLASS

"If you are distressed by anything external, the pain is not due to the thing itself but to your own estimate of it; and this you have the power to revoke at any moment."

~ Marcus Aurelius ~

The struggles that we face come with a purpose that may determine how we are going to overcome it. A test that we all have to go through at some point in our life; the purpose that steers us to move toward our greatness when we endure!

"Consider it all joy, my brethren, when you encounter various trials, knowing that the testing of your faith produces endurance. Your endurance will have a perfect result as that you will be perfect and complete, lacking nothing."

(James 1:2-4)

Our Heavenly Father's mission is not limited to our past mistakes or our circumstances. When life gets us down, and I am sure it sometimes does, we all fall short. But the good thing is, God gently brings us, once again, back in line and He knows we are far from perfect. He brings us back into His fold as a Shepherd whose sheep has gone astray.

Everything that we go through is a test. God knows how much we can handle and will not give us more than we can manage. He cares for you and when you have no one to turn to, no one to care for you, He will continue to be a light in the tunnel, guiding you all the way. A light that will not go dim but shine in the middle of your storm.

"No weapon formed against you will prosper and every tongue that rises in judgement will be punished."
(Isaiah 54:17)

He reminds us in Isaiah 55:11 that:

"So, shall My word be that go forth out of My mouth: it shall not return unto Me void, but it shall accomplish that which I please, and it shall prosper in the thing whereto I sent it."
(Isaiah 55:11)

Because *"our thoughts are not His thoughts nor are His ways our ways,"* His word will not return as a lie, but what He has promised to do in our lives, He will fulfil.

As we reflect on the things we cannot change, we will discover that things are not as bad as it looks. Have you ever found how pointless it is to get stressed and upset over situations that you cannot change? God is in control. He had already planned everything out for us, long before we were in our mother's womb before conception.

God told Jeremiah that He was assigned, reserve and *"appointed as a prophet over the nations"* (Jeremiah 1:5). God will use us for His glory as we become sanctified and separated from sin.

So, when you feel unloved and unwanted, abandoned, neglected and torn apart, remember that **God loves you more than you can imagine**. He is your Father, and He wants the best for you. When you feel 'messed up' and you have nowhere to turn, use every effort to elevate yourself and soar like an eagle, soaring high on the wings of the Lord.

Why do you remain stuck in your circumstances? Do you know that God will do what seems impossible for you? Our faith can move mountains, and by our faith, we may see things in the supernatural.

There were many times when I have felt stuck, not knowing how and when to move from where I was. The years of feeling that way was becoming tiresome and drained. It can be overwhelming when we use the energy to create and speak negative words over our lives. But when we speak life in those dead situations, we will see a new beginning occurring. These dry bones, can they live again? Yes, they can! Every dead situation you speak life to, we will see new life, new beginnings and a future! (Ezekiel 37:1-3).

We are encouraged to pray without stopping and to rejoice always by giving thanks in all circumstances. Likewise, when the feelings of worry, fear and discouragement come, we are encouraged to turn to prayer and thanksgiving and make our request known to God; but not to refrain from praying.

God knows the plans that He has for us. God declared in Jeremiah 29:11 the plans to prosper us and not to harm us and also plans to give us hope and future. He wants to emancipate us from where we are and take us to the next level. Sometimes He allows us to go through the process of life, and while going through the process we can sometimes get slowed down with the wrong decision and bad choices.

While feeling stuck in our mess, our mess will become our message. God is allowing us to make choices that please Him. He will bring us to the place that will change our situation and the circumstances that we may face.

It was through my mess that I experienced the power of God in my life! It was not only the test that I had to endure but my ability to move forward and step into the promise of God.

Should I have had to go through the calamity of my past to see my future? Yes! Your experiences help you to be strong and to understand yourself as God sees you!

Our desire should be for us to arise from where we were to where we are now and step out in God-confidence into our new season! For us to step into a new brand season and enjoy the benefits of God's plan, we have to give to God all our past mistakes, choices and brokenness. But in order to do this, we must recognise that we have made many of those mistakes and choices. Sometimes, we are thrown into situations, but often we are responsible for our circumstances and the decisions that got us there, not someone else. Recognise what you should have taken responsibility for, and own up to your wrong decisions and place them at the feet of the Lord. For everything else, He will take care of it if you ask, in His way, in His time.

~ CHAPTER FOUR ~

In the Midst of Pain

YOUR SONG SHALL BE YOUR STORY

"Out of pain and problems have come the sweetest songs, and the gripping stories."

~ Billy Graham ~

My life was not always a bag of roses over-spilling with fresh smelling fragrance; it was quite the opposite for me, and to be honest, too often the bad outweighed the good.

As humans, we sometimes concentrate on those bad times and illuminate the good things that we had before the hurt. In the midst of the pain, the very thing that keeps us moving in the right direction, in time, will propel us to our greatness. Is that not awesome to know?

If you have been broken-hearted and found there is nothing you can do to control the situation, God is a healer of the broken-hearted. He always looks after his own in a time of crisis. God will not leave us or forsake us; He has our back.

Scriptures reveal not one, but many names for God the Father. His character is revealed throughout the Bible by the descriptive names He chose to create an intimate relationship with His people.

When you need healing, call upon the name:

Jehovah Raphe: The Lord who Heals.
"I will put none of the diseases on you which I have brought on the Egyptians. For I am the Lord, who heals you."
(Exodus 15:26 NKJV)

When you need help, call upon the name:

Jehovah Nissi: The Lord is my Banner.
"Moses built an altar and called it 'The Lord is my Banner.' Because hands were lifted up against the throne of the Lord."
(Exodus 17:15-16)

When you need God for provision call on the name:

Jehovah Jireh: God will Provide
God said to Abraham: *"My son, God will provide for Himself the Lamb for a burnt offering."*
(Genesis 22:8 NKJV)

It does not matter what tomorrow will bring; God will walk into any situations that awaits you in the tomorrows. He is in your tomorrows where His love stretches far beyond our imagination. His ways and understanding remains a mystery to us.

When you need God to show up:

Jehovah Shammah: The Lord is there
"…the name of the city from that day shall be: THE LORD IS THERE."
(Ezekiel 48:35 NKJV)

Your relationship with God should be rooted in His love, so that when you are in the storm of life, *"He will be a present help in times of trouble."*

He will be a place of refuge that protects and strengthens us against the wiles and the devices of the enemy.

When you feel like everyone is against you, call upon the name:

El Elyon; God Most High.
"...blessed be God Most High, Who has delivered your enemies into your hand."
(Genesis 14:19-20 NASB)

Although my pain spanned the last thirty years from my teenage years to adulthood, I was able to lift the burden of the hurt by forgiving those who had wronged me. It was not an overnight thing where one minute I was in shock and then another minute I was blissfully happy.

Everything that we go through is for our good. It is a process and will always begin with forgiveness. In the midst of your storm, move towards finding the love that is needed for your healing, through Jesus Christ.

If you are reading this book and you are in your storm, and cannot find any way out, be patient and wait on God for your breakthrough. The storm may be raging and windy in your situation right now but hold on a little while longer. Although we may face the problematic and challenging battle getting over the obstacles that we face on a daily basis, we have to hold on to dear life to succeed those challenges. Hold on!

When you are feeling bad about yourself, unable to forgive yourself, call upon the name:

Jehovah Mekadesh: The Lord who Sanctifies you.
"You will keep my statutes and practice them.
I am the Lord who Sanctifies you."
(Leviticus 20:8 NASB)

One thing for certain, God knew you before you came out of your mother's womb and He knew your name!

> *"In the womb, I formed you, and I knew you. Before you were born, I consecrated you...."*
> **(Jeremiah 1:5)**

It is hard to understand the emotion a child will feel when they are rejected, hurt and abandoned. Can a mother forget the baby on her breast and show no compassion for her child she gave birth to?

> *"Though she may forget, I will not forget you! See, I have engraved you on the palms of my hands."*
> **(Isaiah 49:15-16)**

God never forgets who you are nor does He stop loving you, even when we turn our backs on Him. He loves you, and His purpose for your life was planned because you are special and blessed. Occasionally, every now and again through our physical pain and our emotions, we have to tread the journey of faith to see the blessings that God has promised us.

You can find joy through your pain. You must not give out on hope. Giving up on hope will be detrimental for your spiritual life. The enemy will find a 'crack' to crawl and squeeze into. He does not need an invitation to disrupt and dismantle your future and the lives of your children. He knows how to 'party crash' into your future without your permission.

> *"He heals the broken-hearted and binds up their wounds."*
> **(Psalm 147:3)**

Do not miss the opportunity to know who God is, in this new season, and why He sent His Son to die for us. When Jesus stretched out His hands on the Cross, He did it for you and for me. He did not reject us, nor did He see fit to come down from the Cross to save Himself, but remained, bruised and beaten for the sake of mankind.

God does not judge us on our shortcomings and failures. So often, we have judged others and their failings, forgetting that God has forgiven us through His grace. He loves us when our mother and father forsake us because His love outweighs our broken and wounded life, as we face up to the pain and receive the joy that He has promised. When we are broken, and in the valley of despair, God always knows when to reposition us and takes us back into the fold of His arm. His love for me was endless even when I made mistakes along the way, and boy, there were many!

So, there I was, broken and alone, I found myself turning to God for help. In my 'midnight hour' I called out to Him through the tears. He helped me in the past, so long ago, and I now wanted Him to do it again. God has never left me, and He has always helped me when I was in distress. But today, I needed Him more urgent than ever. I had run from Him to do my 'own thing' but it all proved too much in the end. I was not in control of my life!

In my later years, as I got older in wisdom and understanding, I realise that my parents, when I was a child, were not given a manual or a blueprint to care for and nurture me effectively. They did not know any better and they did what they knew was best for me. Although I cannot judge my parents or blame them for my past failures and child traumas, I can only forgive them.

Sometimes and more often we find it comfortable, without difficulty, to blame others and not ourselves of our messed-up lives. If you are one of those people who systematically blame others for your misfortune and setbacks; **Get Over It!** No one takes precedence over our future when we have the responsibility to plan our future.

Reflect and think about your past setbacks and the many opportunities that you have lost and encountered. Although you have lost potential opportunities, because of past hurt and resentment with someone who you have held onto unforgiveness, it is never too late to start over. Yes, you have lost the years, but that should not stop you to shine! Shine and sparkle like never before! Start today and forgive everyone who had a 'foot in' your future and thank those people who did not want you to move forward.

As I reflected and thought about past setbacks, and the many opportunities that had passed me by, I was hurt and full of pride to move forward with the unforgiving heart. My heart was sore and bruised and there was nothing God could do! So, I thought!

Joel Osteen once said:

"Too often we sit on the side-lines nursing our wounds. But the God who created the universe is about to pick you up, breathe new life into your dreams, and propel you towards your destiny!"

These verses will remind you that you are not alone, and that God is always present:

1. **God is my Refuge and Strength**, an ever-present help in trouble (Psalm 46:1)
2. Be strong and courageous; **God is with you** wherever you are! (Joshua 1:9)
3. Through the darkest valley, I will not fear evil, **God is with me** (Psalm 23:4)
4. **The Lord is my Light** and my Salvation, who shall I be afraid of? (Psalm 27:1)
5. May God's unfailing love be my comfort (Psalm 119:76).

PRAYER

Father, in the middle of my storm, I need You. I need Your strength when I feel weak and cannot do anything. Let me need You like never before. I need Your directions when I am alone and don't know where to turn to for comfort. Be my Refuge and my Strength when I am in trouble. I ask that Your strength overtakes me when I am low in spirit. Help me to withstand the turmoil of life and what I am about to face. Help me to be strong and courageous. Through my darkest hour, let no fear encamp around me as Your presence empower me. Sometimes I fear the unknown, but I am asking You to remind me that You did not give me "the power of fear but of love and a sound mind," through Your unfailing love. Amen.

~ CHAPTER FIVE ~

Soul Ties

ONE HEART, ONE SOUL, ONE YOKE

"Therefore, shall a man leave his father and his mother, and shall cleave unto his wife: and they shall be one flesh."

(Genesis 2:24)

The definition for Soul Ties: *"It is emotional bondage that ties us to another person that prohibits the individual, in this case the woman, from moving on."* [5]

Godly and ungodly relationships are entwined and interlinked by Soul-ties. Ungodly soul-ties are formed and woven together between two individuals, by contract or on an agreement. God ordains a godly soul-tie under the covenant of marriage. A wrongful understanding of each other can connect us with ungodly soul-ties which may later lead to hurt and brokenness associated with the relationship. However, if the relationship is broken down, sometimes it is the soul-ties that become difficult to remove.

What is brokenness?

There are many factors relating to brokenness which can take on many forms of the definition. It can consist of depression, emptiness, shame, anxiety insignificance, addictions, obsessive thoughts and compulsive behavioural attitude. Although soul-ties is link in with brokenness, Godly soul-ties are, according to the Bible, a principle that is spiritual, where two people have a godly covenant agreement that brings God's purpose into our future. What am I saying?

Matthew 18:19 states:

> *"Again, I say to you, that if two of you agree on earth about anything that they may ask, it shall be done for them by My Father who is in Heaven."*

So, we create Soul-ties when we connect intimately with each other by mutual agreement or contract. As we look more closely at ungodly soul-ties in a compelling way, it can be seen as a contract that binds one to the other in a strong ungodly bond. It is crucial that we are in a correct and rightful relationship with whomever we align ourselves.

Within the younger generation, we can recognise some of the peer pressures that young people are facing in today's society. They are extremely keen to be a part of a movement where they feel wanted; they are looking for a sense of belonging and because of their need to belong, they sometimes find themselves involved in illegal groups, sexual promiscuity and drug-taking activities. This, in fact, can cause detrimental and long-term bondage for the future in relationships and marriages, where spiritual darkness is present.

The results of ungodly ties between two people can be 'spell-binding' which can control our lives and binds us to this spiritual principle. Long-term, Godly soul-ties, such as those that are tied in marriage together in covenant, carries a weight that binds two people together in covenant with each other.

In contrast, ungodly soul-ties, from a particular group of people that have the desire for the same sex, can sometimes cause such persons to be spiritually bound together in the supernatural. Ungodly soul-ties can also be from different partners from all walks of life that a person is not married to but has sexual activities outside of marriage.

Many reasons that may cause a soul tie:

1. When a person, through sex, find themselves involved intimately. A person may sleep with another person purely for sex but later find themselves longing for the other person after sex. They do not have to be connected emotionally with each other, but now a soul tie may have created spiritually.
2. Women generally sometimes fall emotionally into the trap by having sex with someone who they believe to love and care for them. She is doting that the relationship between each other will bond through intimate sex. Often, the woman is the one at the end of the hurt chain that will feel the brunt of rejection. She will find herself connected spiritually through soul ties to someone that she now resent.
3. When two people decide to go through the journey of marriage, in a covenant, they are linked and tied to a healthy soul tie. But if two persons choose to opt out of the commitment of marriage and leave the relationship, the pain and the damage may occur through the breakup of that relationship. The wound of parting is much extensive than that of one that takes advantage of another person.

According to David Cross, director of Ellel Ministries, UK, *"We should let go, cut loose and turn away from the effect of every wrong hold a relationship that is ungodly has on you."* We are reminded that ungodly soul ties are ungodly yoke which can tie or bind us to the person not intended by God.

Godly and ungodly relationships are entwined and interlinked by Soul-ties. Ungodly soul-ties are formed and woven together between two individuals, by contract or on mutual agreement. God ordains a godly soul-tie under the covenant of marriage. A wrongful understanding of each other can connect us with ungodly soul-ties which may later lead to hurt and brokenness associated with the relationship. However, if the relationship is broken down, sometimes it is the soul-ties that becomes difficult to remove.

Men often find it less awkward to give up on a relationship and they seem to move on with more ease than women. That's because women cannot separate sex and love. When we give of ourselves in this way, we bind ourselves unwittingly to that person. So, it is important for us to let go of relationships that keep us tied to ungodly soul-ties. Better yet, it is better not to get involved in that way in the first place.

When in doubt, call upon the name:

Jehovah Rohi: The Lord is my Shepherd.
"The Lord is my Shepherd; I shall not want."
(Psalm 23:1 NASB)

For you to receive God's blessings, you have to make up your mind to hear from God and expect what it is He wants you to do.

In Jeremiah 29:11, "the Lord declares the plans that He has for you." The reason we sometimes go through what we are experiencing, God is setting us up for a new beginning and a new purpose. God is not finished with us, and He is not about to let us go. Let go of the ungodly soul-ties so that God will do a new thing in your new season!

PRAYER

Lord, I pray that the fruit of the Spirit abide in me, as Your Word begin to arise in my heart. Thy words will I hide in my heart because Your thoughts towards me are excellent! Because you have me in your plans, I am always on Your mind. You are turning every evil for my good because You love me. Today, I will receive Your love, because You have created me in the likeness of You. Heal me from any 'parental rejection' or relationship rejection that I may have, as I continue to trust You. Amen.

~ CHAPTER SIX ~

Picking up the Pieces

BRUSH YOURSELF OFF AND START AGAIN

"God, pick up the pieces and put me back together again.
You are my praise!"
(Jeremiah 17:14)

As I picked up the pieces of my troubled and damaged life, I was gaining strength focusing on the positive. I began to notice my smile was coming back and I started to feel happy within myself. It was at that moment I was determined to live my life to the fullest with God's help.

When you are in need or in trouble, remember that God is your refuge and strength; so why should you be afraid?

Fear… it seems to me that fear can become a permanent fixated visitor in your life if you allow it to stay longer than necessary. The fear of moving on was difficult for me since I was in that situation for a long time. Fear had taken over my life temporary and it had to go. Fear knew it had overstayed its welcome. The consequences of the abandonment that I felt those years ago begun to take its toll on my emotions.

Fear became overpowering, and as its grip tightened, I knew that it was a matter of time my relationship with fear would soon end. Fear had to go, and because my gut feeling told me that fear did not know how to let go, fear had become dependent on me and held onto dear life as its grip became tighter. Trusting God with my fears were the only way I was able to rid myself from its grip and move on.

It can be easy for a young person to feel ostracised in society, leaving them feeling inadequate and worthless. The Bible reminds us that the enemy roams around like a roaring lion waiting to devour anyone in his tracks. He is a deceiver of all lies and is subtle in his games, tactics and his ways to deceive us. He wants your future and the future of your children. In particular, our young men who are dying on the streets in relation to the knife crime which have become rampant on our streets. Another reason why the enemy is a deceiver of all lies; He want to destroy our young men future.

You cannot afford to allow the enemy to steer you away from the path that God has planned for us. We must endeavour to stay on the right track at all times.

If you are reading this book because you are waiting on God to do a new thing in your life, you have come to the right place. God is about to shift something in your life so that He will release what He intended for you in the first place. However, it can be easier for us to conform to society when we are hurting, than for us to be who God has called us to.

> "Do not copy the behaviour and customs of this world, but let God transform you into a new person by changing the way you think. Then you will learn to know God's will for you, which is good and pleasing and perfect.
> **(Romans 12:12)**

Do you mimic the behaviour of the world because of society? Or are you "walking by faith and not by sight?" How important are the opinions of other people to how you see yourself? People perspective of you does not define who you are, and it is how you see yourself, that others will see you. The opinions of people do not define who we are. Although your journey may not be similar to the next person; it is important and vital to know yourself and be yourself. Also, to be the best that you are is a powerful tool that you can use as you turn your situation around in a positive way. Today, you can set goals where you want to be in the next twelve months and sticking to it.

When you push your mind for greatness, you will find that success will follow, and you will know that you have arrive to that place. For many of us, we struggle with the pain of rejection and self-hate, what may seem like a long treacherous journey that will never end. Remember that God is in control and will always cancel every evil assignment the enemy has planned for you. He will restore what the enemy has taken from you and far more that you have lost.

When you're looking for strength, need direction in making decisions, feel out of control, or feel battered by the world, call upon the name:

Elohim: Powerful God.
For it is He who created the world and can bring you what you need.
"In the beginning, God created the heavens and the earth."
(Genesis 1:1)

PRAYER

*Father, as I pick up the pieces of my troubled life and step into my destiny, I pray that You will bring me into a place in my life of **joy and abundance**. I pray that when I am in my 'midnight hour' You will be there and in my season my mourning will turn into dancing, and because of Your favour on my life, no one will take my joy from me. This is the day that You have made, and I will rejoice and be glad in it. Amen.*

~ CHAPTER SEVEN ~

The Act of Forgiveness

FORGIVENESS vs A GRUDGE

"We cannot embrace God's forgiveness if we are so busy clinging to past wounds and nursing old grudges."

~ T.D. Jakes ~

Forgiveness. A word that I hold dear to my heart!

One of the roots of bitterness is unforgiveness. Refusing to forgive others is like cutting off your lifeline to your future and your destiny. You can try to move on with your life and be happy and contented, but one day it will come back reminding you that there are people that you need to forgive. We should take every opportunity to rid ourselves of this unwillingness to forgive others. Otherwise, we are assuming ourselves to be perfect, and we all know this is not true. Each of us has something that needs to be forgiven by another. But it is very difficult to forgive others if you have not fully forgiven yourself. You need not do this alone, however. Know that God forgives you and asking for His forgiveness will go a long way to implanting that seed in your mind.

Holding onto grudges will destroy your inner peace and joy. This spirit is a soul destroyer that will stop at nothing to cause havoc and turmoil in your life, your children and your marriage. I have seen families and homes destroyed because of resentment and jealousy through unforgiveness.

Forgiveness is an act of strength that enables us to move on from a situation that you may have encountered at some point in our lives. We often hold on to resentment because it is the only way we think we can get back to the person that has hurt us. But resentment and bitterness only hurt the person who is holding on to it.

Forgiving someone is not comfortable, and because of our ego it prevents us from forgiving. As a Christian, the Holy Spirit enables us to forgive when we don't want to. But the longer you hold on to resentment the harder it will be for you to move on with your life.

We have often prayed, *"…Forgive us our trespasses as we forgive those who trespass against us…"* (Matthew 6:12) But **do** we forgive those who have wronged us? **Do** we hold on to malice as long as we can just to make that person feel the pang of guilt?

A trespass is an act of offence against another person, and if you are expecting to receive God's blessings and forgiveness, you have to learn to forgive. Often the other person does not even know they have offended you.

> *"Therefore, confess your sins to each other and pray for each other so that you may be healed…"*
> **(James 5:16 NIV)**

I have learnt to forgive those who have wronged me and who have misunderstood me in the past. My relationship with my mother is getting better as we learn to understand each other. Also, I, too, had to forgive those that I have wrongly accused in the past.

Writing this book released me of the unwanted emotions that bound my life for years. It was a difficult task I found both emotional and overwhelming. As the fingers began to type the sentences non-stop, tears began to fall for the first time as I remembered my years of damage. Moving on with my life was something I needed to do because I wanted God to forgive me when I did something that was not pleasing to Him.

The sad thing that I have learnt is that when we do not forgive we leave unresolved issues behind when we leave this earth; these issues are left on loved ones who may need your forgiveness and who will not have the opportunity to say, "I forgive you."

Forgiveness brings peace and freedom, and it releases you from the power of that person or situation. The only way that you will know that you have forgiven the person that wronged you is when they walk into the room, and you no longer feel any negative emotions.

Each of us has one life; a life that should be filled with peace and tranquillity instead of anger or resentment. It is impossible to move on and live your life in peace when you have a heart that is not forgiving. Forgiveness brings healing and healing brings joy, and joy brings peace.

The act of forgiveness also brings physical benefits such as lowered blood pressure and heart rate, as well as reducing levels of depression and anxiety. Resentment is self-afflicted, and the person who remains hurt is yourself. In fact, in theory, the person you have the issue with may have moved on with their life over the years, forgetting what the issues was in the first place; and you are still worrying about the past!

> *"But I have raised you up for this very purpose, that I might show you my power and that My name might be proclaimed in all the earth"*
> **(Exodus 9:16)**

In our busiest moments, when we are bustling here, there and everywhere, we can sometimes forget our purpose. We can also forget God's plan and purpose for our lives. As we jog our mind to His promise, we must always remember that God's purpose is always greater than our own.

As you take that step for greatness and recognising how broken you are, you should take a real close-up on what is going on in your inner being. You do not have to be ashamed of your brokenness because many of us are silently going through it. Sometimes as women we hold on to past hurt and resentment and we try not to talk about it because we are ashamed of our past hurt and we are afraid to 'tell people our business.' However, by keeping it locked inside of you, or never telling anyone or sharing it as your testimony, you deny someone else's freedom to receive their victory.

> *"We know that in ALL things God works for the good of those who love Him, who have been called according to His purpose."*
> **(Romans 8:28)**

The Power of Purpose

Have you ever wondered what it would be like not having a purpose, having no hope? Why am here? What is my purpose for being here?

Some years ago, I found myself wondering about my purpose. There was many questions that I have asked myself, 'what my purpose is.' Growing up in Church did not teach me this, nor did it give me the information that I needed to pursue my goals, and often, as young teenagers, they will go elsewhere to find the answers to their questions. I found no answers to my questions.

Although I was not a Christian, after I had left home, I often felt there was no significant reason to be here. 'Here today and gone tomorrow' was my answer to everything. However, my life journey, since leaving home, began to change my perspective on life and the Creator. It also dawned on me, some years later, that I was here for a purpose and that God made a way for me to obtain the understanding of Him and why I was here.

Sometimes we can feel discouraged and rejected by current situations that we are not in control of. Regardless how we feel about God and your lack of knowledge; He remain to love us unconditionally. We may not acknowledge Him as the Father over our lives, but He is always there in the times that we need Him.

Through your experiences of life, and the obstacles that have always prevented you from moving forward can propel you to your greatness! Waking up in the mornings and having a purpose keep us motivated every day. Without a purpose, life can be a drag and a soul destroyer.

Your identity in Christ Jesus gives us the understanding and the purpose to push until we see something happen. Your purpose and your zeal will elevate you where no one would of thought it was possible, despite the negative words that may have spoken over your life.

Find your purpose today. Everyone has a purpose, but it is how we tap into it and find the missing link to where our focus and future lies. Your future lies within you and only you will discover what it is that is hidden within you. Read books that will give you information about self-development and pray about it so that God will give you direction to make the right decisions.

Do not feel stressed or anxious when you are not doing your best! **Be the best you!** Always remember the **why** and trust the **who** and one day the **how** will reveal itself.

You may, like me, have wanted to write a book but do not know how to proceed to the next step. You have a book within you to share to the world and to bless and encourage others. It was because of my purpose to write that I found other writers who shared their story to the world so that they can release the healing. Wounded hearts, brokenness, molestation, rape, rejection and other painful situations has prompted authors to tell their story.

What Prompted Me to Tell My Story?

My God-given purpose prompted me to write my story so that others like you can be set free from your hurt emotions. I wanted to let people know that they do not have to be stuck where they are. You are not alone, and there is someone out there that are going through the same situation. But there is hope.

When we are hurt, we always think we are the only person who are going through it. It seems impossible to identify the same struggles that someone else is going through what you have been through and survive! But finding what your purpose is and following your dreams will see new doors opening. To be vulnerable is to find ways to release yourself from the pain and past hurt. What you can do to activate the purpose, you have to start somewhere closer to home – You!

How do we respond to the promise that God has promised us?

First, you must locate the promise in the Word because the Word of God covers every situation that you are facing. How you respond to the promise is to plant a seed in the Word. The Word is life to you when you seek after the promise of God. So, whatever is happening in your life right now, your finances, your marriage, your children or your job opportunities, let the Word be your strong Tower. Read every promise of Truth in every situation you are going through, go into the Word and speak life in your circumstances.

"When you get the Word, you get God in the situation"
~ Creflo Dollar ~

Every struggle that comes your way comes as a purpose to steer you to your greatness. It moves us towards success in which is lined with the plan of God. Our past does not define God's purpose, or current situation, nor is He limited by our lack of knowledge of Him. But knowing who you are, and your purpose will make a difference to what you choose to become. Sometimes we have to 'bite the bullet' and do it anyway.

Failure can sometimes play a significant role in our reluctant to finding our purpose. Our negative response to how we feel about ourselves do not leave room to grow. We self-sabotage and speak negative things over our life because we stop believing in ourselves. We take on the persona of someone's negative perspective of us and wear it like a cloak of many colours. We will always have failures, but how we respond to it will make a difference.

When life itself begins to take a toll on us you should only look up and know that you have a Saviour! By looking up to God, it will remind you that you are not far from Him, and that His right hand will hold you up in times of trouble. Did you know that we all fall short of His glory? When we stray a little, God gently brings us, once again, back into line. We are far from perfect. But one thing for sure, everything that we may face will challenge us to step out of our comfort zone.

"Forget the former things; do not dwell on the past. See I am doing a new thing."
(Isaiah 43:18)

The former things that we so often dwell on are in the past. God is doing a new thing in your season. This is your season to shine and sparkle and be the best that you are. We are not excused from receiving the victory and the blessings that He is able to give us. The things of the past are gone, but not forgotten. It is the past experiences which may drive you to do better as you step into your purpose and destiny.

Yes, the former things are gone, and everything will become new in this season of your life. If God can do it for me, He will do it for you. He is no respecter of persons nor does His Word come back void!

PRAYER

Father, help me to be who You called me to be. Help me not to hold on to resentment and bitterness that will stop me from receiving the promise that You have planned for me. I know that You are working everything for my good and I trust You with my decisions, my life and my plans. I pray that you will create in me a new heart and renew a righteous spirit within me.

Help me to forgive those who have wronged me, be it my friends, relationships or my family. Because of my past hurt and disappointment, I pray that you will forgive me if I have blamed You for my misfortunes and mishaps that I may have placed or invited in my life.

Remove any bitter savour of resentment, pain, mistrust, and importantly, rejection from me so that I can live my life in abundance in Jesus' name. Amen!

~ CHAPTER EIGHT ~

Taking a Stand Against Fear

TO OVERCOME FEAR IS TO BE FREE
"He who has overcome his fears will truly be free."
~ Aristole ~

At the age of twelve, I first encountered fear. What I did experienced was a sudden reaction mixed with an overwhelming feeling of dread and dismay. It was an emotion that came out of the ordinary for me. It was an issue that would control my mind set! You see, the mind-set has to take a positive turn to make a full recovery for you to feel the joy that God has given to you. Fear comes to destroy your will to live, and it comes to keep you in a box and never fulfilling your purpose.

When you look at the word 'Fear', you can, in an instant, relate to what it means, primarily because it affects you in a personal way. Fear can only be eliminated when we trust and believe that God will help us to get over it.

> *"The Lord is on my side; I will not fear:*
> *What can man do to me?"*
> **(Psalm 118:6)**

What is fear? Fear is False Evidence Appearing Real and the emotions which are caused by the feeling of being threatened. Sadly, many of us are walking around day after day with fear, and it has become a part of us. We are afraid to move on and accomplish what our future self is telling us to do. Fear of forgiving someone who has hurt us and fear of letting go of a toxic relationship because of fear of rejection.

But the Bible states that:

> *"There is no fear in love [dread does not exist], but full grown [complete, perfect] love turns fear out of the door and expel ever trace of terror! For fear "brings with it the thought of punishment, and [so] he who is afraid has not reached the full maturity of love [is not yet grown into love's complete perfection]"*
> **(1 John 4:18 AMP)**

Perfect love that reminds us that God loves us, and whatever your shortcomings are, He loves you. In our mess, He loves and desire us to have a life full of joy in abundance. When we hide behind a 'happy face' to self-protect ourselves from the eyes of others, our response is to seek God's help. Sooner or later the anxiety of fear, if unresolved, will controlled you in the end but if we position or change our mind-set from the control of doubt, it will no longer be our master or our controller. Boldness should be the epiphany to cast out fear, because in the end it will destroy and sabotage your destiny.

In relationships or marriage, we can become fearful of the possibility of our spouse committing infidelity or fear that they may leave the marital home. Sometimes we can spend our whole life being afraid of

At the age of thirty-four, I forgave my mother. I was now released from unforgiveness and had returned to Church, despite the Church wound I had not forgotten.

My first encounter with my spiritual side came as the desire for something bigger than myself became strong. There were some days that I would turn the television on to listen to a television Pastor droning on about forgiveness and salvation. It was through that moment of receiving my healing when I heard the message he told the congregation if they want to receive forgiveness from God, they would have to forgive others who have done wrong to them. I listened very intently to the message. It was at that moment I knew that God was trying to tell me something.

Too often God is shouting in our ears to get our attention, but we are so busy doing other things, or nursing a harden heart that we cannot hear Him. Forgiving my parents, especially my mother, spiritually released my breakthrough. It helped me to move on with my life, and God was able to work in my heart by cleansing me from the debris of rejection and hurt. If you could experience what forgiving a person does to you, it would never take you that long to forgive others.

When the television Pastor told his congregation that God loves us unconditionally, this was my cure from self-blaming. I discovered God's love for the first time, and it has helped me to rediscover my relationship with Him and take the necessary steps of recovery.

When you're looking for peace in your life, call upon the name:

Jehovah Shalom: The Lord is Peace.
*"So, Gideon built an altar there to the Lord,
and called it The-Lord-Is-Peace"*
(Judges 6:24 NKJV)

the things around us, and before you know it, we have wasted years that we cannot get back.

At the age of twelve years old, I felt afraid of the thunderstorm. It would sometimes bother me when the thunder and lightning appeared, especially in the nights or the early mornings. Some nights, I would find myself reading a book. I found enjoyment in reading a book a day or more. In fact, my books were my friends! So, when everyone played outdoors and socialised with friends, my book and I were the perfect company, and oh, it was indeed my friend!

One night as I lay awake, it was a thundery night full of lightning and noise. A noise that would not stop. I can remember it as if it was yesterday. As the rain beat down on the window, it became difficult for me to read or go to sleep because of the disturbing noise of the storm. Beside me in the bed, my sister, who was eleven months older, was asleep as we both shared a room together, being one of the oldest of six siblings. As she lay in the bed snoring, her snoring became louder with the thunder and rain, and I could not but wish I was sleeping through this awful night, almost envying her. Everyone in the house was asleep. As I became restless with fear, I began to feel afraid that the thunder and lightning were going to get the better of me. As the rain beat against my window, I was petrified. I nudged my sister to wake up because I needed her awake so that I can have the company while experiencing the storm. But she grunted and went back to sleep. The noise was now getting louder and louder and nothing that I could do to stop the rain.

I remember saying to God that if He would stop the thunder and rain, I would give my life to Him. It was in that instance I had my prayer answered. As I had uttered those words from my mouth, the thunder stopped! It was that instant! It was no coincidence or magic, but it was the power of God at work.

God had heard me and answered my prayer. My faith in that instant was stronger than before, and I knew that God was a God that listened.

We all go through storms in our lives, and sometimes we have to go it alone when the wind and the rain and the tsunami weather are beating down fast. You can experience different wintry seasons, but you can be an overcomer during the storm. This gives us assurance of the many blessings that we are going to receive as God works in our lives. Therefore, your situation may be as high as a mountain, but you have to allow God to work in your heart as He calms the storm. There will be times you will have to trust God for directions. It will not be easy but remember that He is our Helper in the times when we are in trouble. There is nothing that He cannot do for us.

Fear is not meant to excel you, nor is it intended for you to get to the next level in God or move forward in your destiny. Ultimately, if we allow fear to be our friend or soulmate, it will eventually find ways to prevent you from living your purpose. Sadly, many have become fearful to go out and reach for their destiny or begin the work that God has given them. Fear has crippled many of us, because we are afraid to launch out into the deep in our destiny, our dreams or our ministry. Is fear preventing you from living your dreams? Or is it becoming an obstacle or your giant? You have to find a way to combat fear because it is a spirit that will not care how you progress. Fear will become your friend and keep you in bondage, leaving you afraid to do anything. But God is still on the throne when we are in doubt and when we do not know the answers. He will never leave us nor forsake us in our time of need.

My mother had always told me that the thunder represented God's anger towards me. The fear of knowing this was extremely upsetting to me as a child. Why would God be punishing me when I did wrong? This was a God who sent His only begotten Son to the Cross to die for me. A God that loved unconditionally and through His grace that is sufficient for me. So why would God want me to be afraid and live my life in fear? Fear is a tormenting spirit that has nothing to do with God.

My mother was fearful of the thunder and not realising, she neutralised this negative notation on me.

Some years later, I began to have a flashback of the thundery noise, and I remembered that night when I was twelve. I prayed that same prayer, but differently this time. I longed to receive deliverance from fear and never for it to return to me again, especially the fear of thunder.

God answered my prayer, and as I got older, the thunder had not bothered me again. I am fear-free, free from the bondage of fear surrounding thundery nights or days.

> *"Do not fear [anything], for I am with you; do not be afraid, for I am your God. I will strengthen you, be assured I will help you; I will certainly take hold of you with My righteous right hand [a hand of justice, of power, of victory, of salvation]."*
> **(Isaiah 41:10)**

Declarations that combats fear:

1. 2 Timothy 1:7 – **"God did not give us a spirit of fear but of power and of love and of a sound mind."**

   Fear will become active and have the power to control you and your emotions. Every obstacle that the enemy has planned for you is linked to fear. God has given you the power to break the spirit of fear that have crippled you for so long. This kind of fear can only be destroyed though prayer and fasting.

2. Galatians 5:1 MEV) – **"For freedom Christ freed us, but therefore stand fast and do not be entangled again with the yoke of bondage."**

   Christ has freed you from all unrighteousness as you surrender to His will and break the bondage of fear on your life. God has given you the power and authority to overcome the enemy.

3. Isaiah 10:27 MEV – **"In that day his burden shall be taken away from off your shoulder, and his yoke from off your neck; and the yoke shall be destroyed because of the anointing oil."**

   Fear will choke your dreams, your destiny and the plans of the future. The anointing will break and destroy every yoke that hangs around your neck and it will dismantle the plans of the enemy as He sets you free from the bondage of fear. But nothing is impossible for God, as He protects you and heal the pain that caused fear.

~ CHAPTER NINE ~

Hope for a Better Place

FINDING HOPE IN THE FACE OF FEAR

"We must accept finite disappointment, but never lose infinite hope."

~ Martin Luther King, Jr ~

How many times have we asked God for something, and when it does not happen we give up and do our own thing? Waiting is a process where we trust and believe that God will do what He promised. His words do not come back void nor is He a man that lies. *"His word will remain in my heart as a burning fire, a fire shut up in my bones"* (Jeremiah 20:9NIV).

As we wait patiently with anticipation, God will reveal to us what we never could have believed: that we made it through! I was amazed that God turned my situation around! God loves you with an everlasting love, and each of us are equally, using the same measure, according to our needs and His will.

For you to have a better and prosperous life and be at peace with yourself, you must aim to put God first in all things before your own priorities. You must avoid spending time and energy assuming, when things do not work out as it should, that you have failed. Failure is not your potion nor is failure your middle name. In order to become who, you were created to be, you have to remain focus on what you **can** do, not on what you **cannot** do.

To become a successful leader, you have to be in the circle of successful and like-minded people who are going places! Although we conjure up different excuses, at some point you need to get off the fence and put faith into practice.

Having a plan in place will illuminate the problems as they arise, the problems that we experience from day to day. Having a plan will allow you to work around and through problems because you are sticking to your plan; you are able to put in writing what needs to be done to get from point A, where you are now, to point B, where you want to go or what you want to achieve. We can never foresee every problem that might arise, so any plans should be flexible enough to be adjusted when those unforeseen problems arise. Have faith in yourself and maintain your vision, because vision and destiny are just a faith away. We can only pray that we focus on the things above and on God's plan for us.

So why should **you** make a plan when God clearly has a plan for you? Because you can't just sit in a sinking boat and wait to be rescued. You must do your own part, take an active role in your own life, and keep your eye on what feels right, what you intuit as being within God's plan for you. If something you've planned hits negativity in ways that are causing you to go uphill all the time, it's probably not within His will. You are fighting against the tide. You will know, you will feel when something is right, when the direction you are taking is the right one. Listen to your heart and your instincts. This is God showing you the way.

My rejection has been my building pad for elevation; the foundation God has built for me. God's love remains forever and ever, and it does not change with time or situation. It is unconditional, and God will be consistent with His love because of His faithfulness towards us. He is our eternal Father who knows what is best for us.

So, why was I allowed to be cast out of my home as a teenager? How can this be seen as God's plan for me? There can be many paths to the same destiny. Perhaps I would have been shown a different path had I been allowed to grow up at home, but my mother made a mistake. Her spirit was troubled, and she ended up throwing me out. But God, who turns all things for good, honed me in adversity and I was still shown the path to repent.

God is Love, and those who love Him will love Him in Spirit and in Truth. He has gone to prepare a place for us and where He is, there we will also be. So, if perfect love drives or casts out fears, why should we be restless for the future?

> *"I trust in the Lord with my heart and soul; I will not lean on my understanding."*
> **(Proverbs 3:5)**

When Words Are Not Enough

> *"Let us not love in word, neither with the tongue; but with deed and truth."*
> **(1 John 3:18)**

"If ever, in a time as this, that I have desired from the Lord, this I will continue to seek after and dwell in the Sanctuary of the Lord and to look on the beauty of the Lord as I seek after Him in His Temple." **6**

As we face different adversaries, God is allowing us to move to the next level. We will experience God's unmerited love and grace He has made available for us.

After all that you may have been through in the past and have survived so many adverse situations, God's plan will work in your favour. Plans to elevate you to be the best that you are.

Toxic friends who have been in your circle will now have been put aside as God continues to sow into your life. Despite all that you have been through, God will release His love into your life. As a result, you will be set free from the obstacles and the bondages of fear that caused you to think that you were not loved. You were loved!

I realise that I had kept my teenage years locked away deep inside and many times, I had tried so hard to remember events in the past, whether unfavourable or positive, but was unable to remember. But God had a plan for me. As I write this book, floods of events, prior to my sudden departure from my home, came to my memory!

Words cannot describe how I am feeling at this moment. It feels so unreal when I think of where I was and where I am now; my heart leaps with delight. The joy that I feel is more than words I can ever express.

As I launch out into the deep and took up the challenge to follow my dreams I began to see doors opening for me. It was my year to shine and sparkle like never before. Who would have thought that I would end up writing this book for you and the many people that are going through what I have been through? Although they are many who have gone through more trivial situations, I thank God that all that I have been through, *"He is able to do exceedingly and immeasurable more than all we can ask or imagine, according to His power that is at work within us"* (Ephesians 3:20 NIV).

I had made myself available for God to use me. God was taking me through a process I did not understand. The process was not natural to me, and it has been so difficult at times, but due to His unmerited love for me, God has always had my back. God will always have your back when you are faced with obstacles or trials that you cannot control. What He has done for me He will do the same for you and for anyone who asks and believes.

> *"The weapon of our warfare is not carnal but mighty through God to the pulling down of the stronghold"*
> **(2 Corinthians 10:4)**

The battle is not yours but the Lords!

Sometimes towards the end of the battlefield, you may feel as though you are being pulled and shoved around; exhausted with negative energy. But God is more than enough, and when we take the limits off Him, we will see things happening in the supernatural.

> *"A thousand shall fall at thy side, and ten thousand at thy right hand; but it shall not come nigh thee."*
> **(Psalm 91:7)**

You Are Beautiful

> *"Your beauty should not come from outward adornments, such as elaborate hairstyles and the wearing of gold jewellery or fine clothes. Rather, it should be that of your inner self, the unfading beauty of a gentle and quiet spirit, which is of great worth in God's sight"*
> **(1 Peter 3:3-4)**

Who said that we cannot love ourselves and be beautiful at the same time? We are beautifully and wonderfully made by God, through love!

Our beauty should come from within us and not places of adornments such as our expensive clothes and attire. The unfading beauty should be evident from within and should exude a gentle and quiet spirit which is worthy in God's eyes.

A mother who is awaiting the arrival of her baby as the infant hears the heartbeat and the warmth of the mother as the she waits in anticipation of the delivery. It is incredible that one as small as a child can know the difference between being loved and feeling unloved. Looking up into the eyes of the mother, the child finds contentment in her arms. As the child begins to grow and is nurtured correctly with love, the child takes on another persona, knowing his or her parents have good intentions for them. They have taken the direction from their much-loved father and mother, who are praying that their child's decisions make them successful teenagers and adults.

Let us flip the coin from a child who is loved to a child who does not have the same benefit of love. As the unloved child enters into the world, their mother may, more or less, feel the bond and compassion for the new baby at first. The emotions felt by the child can take on the persona of the mother from the umbilical cord and through the birth canal, whether those emotions are happy or negative. Something may have happened along the way, from conception to the birth or after that, during the first three months, or even farther into the child's early formative years.

A child who feels unloved, ugly and not beautiful, may experience fear, loneliness and rejection. More or less they will also feel the anguish with inner pain they may not know how to explain it.

A young child may not know how to deal with these negative feelings and subsequently the only thing that is on their mind is wanting to feel loved.

In my experience, a child who is not loved will grow up with negative feelings of rejection from peers, siblings and people around them, even if they are unwarranted. Trusting someone will be challenging and those feelings, in time, will be reflected onto the relationships they may have in the future. A child who is unloved and unwanted will not feel the same as a child who is loved.

A child who is loved will be more likely to feel beautiful and wanted by people around them. They will also have a better ability to love themselves and recognise the inner beauty they have because they are loved. As parents, we have a duty to our children, although we may have made countless mistakes on the way, to tell them they are beautiful both inside and outside.

My parents were from the Caribbean, so I was raised in a Caribbean lifestyle. I grew up in an era when nurturing was sometimes at the bottom of the list of priorities and many children and even spouses were treated badly.

If you look at the background of your parents and how they received their discipline and nurturing, you might not be surprised to learn that their parenting style is very similar to how they were raised. They became parents and faced the difficulties of giving the child the love that they did not receive themselves. Unfortunately, we see many young people who have left home, not having the real relationship with their parents because of past hurt that remains scarred. Many have not made any contact with parents over many years, and this has kept them from moving on and growing spiritually and emotionally.

If this is you and you have gone through these difficulties and are afraid to admit to it, you are not alone. There are many people like yourself who has had to carry this weight of burden for so long. Maybe you have hidden it at the back of your subconscious and are afraid to take it to the forefront. Today you will surrender it to God to work it out. Nothing is too big for Him to do and you will find that your burden will be lifted. Take the leap of faith and trust God and believing that He will do what He said He will do.

~ CHAPTER TEN ~

Finding Joy Through the Pain

THE JOY OF THE LORD IS YOUR STRENGTH

"Not only so, but we also glory in our sufferings, because we know that suffering produces perseverance; perseverance, character; and character, hope"

(Romans 5:3-5)

It is essential that we forgive ourselves first in order to heal our mind. Any thoughts that may obsruct our intention to move on with our lives should be immediately dismissed. You may find these old feelings resurfacing, which can cause all forms of mental issues, anxiety and pain to resurface.

The mind will always replay what it knows, reinforcing events and ideas that have taken place in your life. To the mind, even thoughts are real; the mind believes what you think about most and because those negative events from your past were coupled with strong emotion and you tend to 'rethink' them often, they remain real. To the mind, every time you think about a negative event, it's as though it is happening right now, the moment you think it.

Whenever those negative emotions, feelings or thoughts resurface, dismiss them and replace them with a positive image. Eventually, your mind will see more positive than negative. Your outlook and behaviour will change as you replace positive thinking in your life.

> *"The Lord is my strength and shield. I trust Him with all my heart. He helps me, and my heart is filled with joy. I burst out in songs of thanksgiving"*
> **(Psalms 28:7)**

Many of the problems that we face in our adult lives are not the ones that determine our destiny; it is when we forgive our parents, peers and relationships of the hurt that we have suffered at their hands that we will find inner strength and peace.

But you must move even farther past forgiveness. You must find something good about those relationships to replace the negative experiences you encountered with them. If there is absolutely nothing good to find, it's okay to pretend, make something up. You can 'see' yourself playing with your father or sibling, for example, laughing and having fun. At some point, this, too, will reflect on your relationship with them.

Every obstacle that you face will be easier to overcome when you let go of past issues and hurt. The past has gone and will never come back, except in your mind, if you let it. It is in your best interest to take each waking moment forgiving loved ones daily so that you can be free to live again!

When I look back and think of the wasted years I spent blaming my mother for the wrong decision she made for my future, it amazes me. Time does not wait for anyone to make that decision to move on, and the years you spend blaming others are years you are being unproductive in your own spirit.

The decision to move on will not be easy, but the layers of our lives are like onions; peel away its layers and you will find a new you! A new you that has been created by the renewing of your mind. A beautiful you from the inside and outside. You will be the portrait of what you were before the hurt that you have carried all those years; a beautiful you!

Finding joy in the midst of pain can be powerful. The Bible reminds us that God will give His angels charge over us in the middle of our storm. He will never leave you even when you think He is far away from you; because the joy of the Lord is your strength.

The Bible also teaches us that as much as we may feel fearful, we have to move on and let go. His love will cause Him to walk on water to rescue us, and He will also calm the storms when they are blowing to and fro. It is amazing what love can do when pain succumbs to joy in the middle of our situations. You have to be careful who you allow to steal your joy, and many times we allow people to enter our lives and give our joy to them; literally give it away!

> *"...weeping may endure for a night, but joy cometh in the morning"*
> **(Psalm 30:5 KJV)**

God loved us enough to send His Son to die for us and bring a new Covenant so that we can be free of sin! Isn't that so amazing! Who can ever do all that He has promised? Only God!

Children at times, learn from the things they see their parents doing, and we often see many teenagers role-playing what they have seen and heard.

Love is a beautiful thing to have because the joy that you feel when being loved is so incredible and indescribable. It breaks all barriers and filters through to us so we can really enjoy life. The Bible states that we should love those whom we see in order for us to love Him! How can we love God whom we cannot see and hate the people that we know!

The Bible states in Joel 3:10: "Let the weak say, **I AM STRONG!**"

As you meditate on this verse, you will know that there is no mention of us declaring that we are weak. But it tells us that we are to decree and claim that **"YOU ARE STRONG!"**

We all go through periods when life seems as if nothing is going our way, but when we are at our weakest, the Bible encourages us to say we are strong.

Sometimes we allow these negative thoughts to enter our minds when we are at our weakest, which in turn draws in more defeat; remember the mind believes what you tell it to believe! Turn it around today!

As we send out words of encouragement to each other in the direction we want our lives to go, we are reminded that we have to build each other in love. Those words encourage us and strengthen us to move forward in positive ways.

Have you ever noticed how a negative person can make everyone around them feel miserable? If you're having a really bad day at work, for example, doesn't it seem as though there's a gloomy atmosphere around you? You are reflecting your feelings. As you encourage others through love, you are reflected upon. In other words, what you give you get. Your love for others is reflected off them back to you.

A report of victory is released now in the atmosphere:
I AM Blessed
I AM Healthy

I AM Prosperous

I AM the Head and not the Tail

I AM more than a Conqueror

I AM a Lender and not a Borrower

I AM Above and not Beneath

I AM ....

The favour of God is on your life! His Strength is made perfect in our weakness! Let the redeemed of the Lord say so!

As you continue to use the **"I AM"** positively, you will move forward to the strength that is made perfect in your weakness through God! He loves us unconditionally, and it does not matter how many wrongs that we have done, nor the failures we receive; Jesus loves us!

I am excited on what God is planning for your life as you make the decision to move forward **from pain to joy**!

What are your 'I Ams'?

_____
_____
_____
_____
_____
_____
_____
_____
_____

Write a report of victories that you have achieved. Think about them. They do not have to be large victories, but every victory however small and insignificant you think they are:

~ CHAPTER ELEVEN ~

Finding Peace

YOUR CIRCUMSTANCES DOES NOT DEFINE WHO YOU ARE

"Inner peace begins the moment you choose not to allow another person or event to control your emotions"

~ Pema Chodron ~

Every day is a work in progress where we take each waking moment that God has given us to assess or evaluate our shortcomings. Life's situations have a way of creeping up when we least expect it and the only way that you can move forward is to boldly take life by the throat, shake out what doesn't belong and reach out to where your destiny lies!

Your failures, accomplishments and goals are the things that will steer you to where your destiny lies. But you must see your failures for what they are, not as something horrible but as a stepping stone to the next stage of your life. Your accomplishments should be written down so you can refer to them when you are feeling as though you can't accomplish anything. And your goals should also be written so when you encounter obstacles, you can get yourself back on track. Only when you tighten the grip on your long-term goals will you find your footing and get back on the path that will lead you to your happiness.

By keeping a positive mind-set, you will be able to stay focused on the desire of your heart. I have learnt late in life that we must change how we think about ourselves. The obstacles that we may face are only temporary. They will not be obstacles for long because everything that we do should be in line with our goals, whether those goals are to get yourself to work on time every day or to start your own business or to make a complete turnaround in a broader area of your life.

Let us come before Him with arms wide open to receive from God His blessing which will be a light unto our feet.

> "The peace of God [the gentle peace that flows from His side] that surpasses all understanding, shall keep you hearts and minds [will equip us with the desires of our hearts; will protect your hearts and minds] in Jesus Christ."
> **(Philippians 4:7 AMP)**

We are not to be anxious about foolishness, and any opportunity that we may have, we are to fervently pray and give thanks and give all of our prayers to Him. It is there we will get the full understanding of God and His promise to us.

Finding peace will put us in a place of inner calmness and meekness within our hearts and mind. Sometimes we have to find time to declutter our minds from the years of negative thoughts, foolishness and mishaps that have so long held us captive.

In the years when my life was not at the place, when I was alone and afraid, it was difficult for me to find the peace that I so much yearned for. My life had become a mess and I often found myself in the grip of fear. In my despair, I sank low in spirit and found no rest, not aware that God was always there to comfort me. It is a great feeling knowing that everything that I had gone through was not my fault nor was it anything to do with me. The guilt that I had held on to in my mind was now releasing its power over me.

God had a plan as He was helping me to release My Story! He was preparing a rebirth; a story to encourage someone that may have gone through what I went through or worse. It is my desire to allow you to read my testimony – that the God that loves you will not allow you to remain in your mess.

Joseph came to mind as I write my story. The Bible tells us in Genesis 37:3-36 that his brothers were nasty to him, even sold him into slavery because of the favour he was shown by his earthly father, Jacob. However, Joseph was put through trial so that he could one day save his family from famine. What a brilliant plan! And one that could never have happened had these men tried to plan it on their own!

Oh, how they laughed and mocked him with his coats of many colours. But what they did not know was that God had a plan for his life, despite what the enemy may say to us. The enemy comes to steal and destroy and will not stop at anything until he deceives us. As a reminder, we have to remain rooted and grounded in His love to withstand the darts the enemy will throw at us from all angles!

Jesus came to redeem the world and, because of His love for us, He went to the Cross alone. He sacrificed His life for one that was so wretched and wicked, just so that we may live.

After years of asking God silently to help my wounded heart, He made a way for me out of nowhere, giving me a breakthrough. That breakthrough to me was a rebirth of who I was in Christ. Many of us feel that way, lonely, rejected, ridiculed, and ostracised by people on a regular basis. Sometimes all you can do at that moment is to cry to your Heavenly Father for forgiveness and mercy.

God – the Author and Finisher of Your Faith

Have you ever felt you cannot go on? Well, I have many times felt that way, broken, bruised, messed up and rejected and left for dead in a world that did not welcome me with open arms. I was left to be swallowed up by the world and saw no way through what I was enduring. But God! He is the finisher of our faith. When you confront to the issues of life and come to see another fulfilled moment of peace and tranquillity, we know that God is working in our lives. The Bible warns us that when we do not look to the Source from where comes our help, we will remain lost in the process of life as it is randomly thrown at us, swimming against the tide with no purpose in mind but to merely survive.

Everything that has happened to me was for a reason that was not in my control. It was a process that God's plan has reflected in my ministry, my walk with Him and everything that is around me.

His tender mercy has taken me through another season of my life although while going through my mess, I was not aware of the process that God had planned for me. Although I was not aware of it at the time, my relationships with other people in my walk in life, my children and my future were a part of the process, and God knew that in time, these people and all the events that surrounded me, negatively, would fulfil His plan in my life. I believe that God was preparing me for the future despite what I had been through.

Have you ever felt the need to ask God, 'Why, God, why?' It just seemed the right question to ask with all what was going on in my life.

In the course of me arriving at a point of my life, I suddenly accepted the need to do something about it! No more procrastination, no more standing at the back bench looking from the side-line at someone else's success. Enough was enough; I was going to do something about it before I got swallowed by the waves of life's issues.

Since writing this book, I have discovered that the pivotal event that kept me in bondage was the rejection by my mother and my departure from my family home at the age of seventeen.

Painful as it seems, God's plan for my life was for me to release all power from this spirit of bondage which held me down for so long! It was my year to shine where everything and every opportunity that I faced would become another stepping stone to get me to where I longed to be; fulfilling my dream! It has taken me this long to get here, but we are not in control of time and time will always reveal what is necessary to us.

I had to do away with pride, self-pride and an undisciplined mind. Each step became more precise and more comfortable as I took baby steps to releasing what God had prepared for me in the future. My past does not determine where I am, but it has helped me to grow stronger, to live boldly and know I am valued. Yes, valued!

How have you found peace in the midst of your turmoil? If yes, write them down:

_____
_____
_____
_____
_____
_____
_____
_____
_____
_____
_____
_____
_____
_____
_____
_____
_____
_____
_____
_____
_____
_____
_____
_____
_____
_____
_____

~ CHAPTER TWELVE ~

Thinking Ahead

IT IS TIME TO BE WHO YOU ARE
We are ALL designed for greatness. No excuses. No apologies."
~ Lisa Nichols ~

There are times when we have to take the necessary steps to move in the direction of our vision. Life's disappointment will come, but we have to find a way to remain focused as we think ahead. It may be hard as we try to make the right decisions to help us move forward, and although we cannot see the future, we can be prepared for what lies ahead. Everything happens to us for a purpose, and you were destined to grow and flourish by your past experiences and the circumstances you faced.

Too often, we live in fear of judgment from the tongues of others in our surroundings; we are unable to move forward. The words spoken negatively over our life can get stuck in our mind and keep us stuck in our thoughts, those same negative thoughts that keep repeating themselves over and over again, preventing us from looking ahead or seeing ourselves from a healthy perspective.

I can recall now as a young teenager alone in the big wide world, that my understanding of who I was at the time, and my reluctance to grow, was measured by my perspective of any faults and mistakes that I had made, and the negative words spoken over my life. What I thought were my capabilities or rather lack of capability, which I had based my life on, was a lie. Everything that I once knew, negatively, was a lie; a lie that prevented me from looking ahead.

We often find ourselves in this dilemma when we have nothing to show for our life, and because our progress, or that which we are called to do, is limited by our own negative self-image, thinking ahead is not a part of the mind-set. All we know is what we see – failure and rejection, hurt and pain, a person without resources or help with nowhere to turn except to the very people who are hurting us. Sometimes, in our need to be needed, we go back to the same people because, in our distorted perception, we believe they 'accept' us. It is a crying shame when we see many people going down the same spiral in their life because of a lack of knowledge about what is available to them.

> *"Good planning and hard work lead to prosperity, but hasty shortcuts lead to poverty"*
> **(Proverbs 21:5)**

Finding God was the best thing that could have ever happened to me, and it could not have come at a better time in my life. His love was poured into me and I found peace that caused me not to never doubt His love. My understanding became clearer with the knowledge of God. The God I know is not the same God my mother knew when I was a teenager.

In the areas of our lives, when our life can be overcome with grief and loss, God can be the High Tower where we can run and be saved. His enduring love touches every area of our life that we deem as unreachable.

> *"Trust in the Lord with all your heart, and lean not on your own understanding."*
> **(Proverbs 3:5)**

As we struggle to look ahead (and there will be times that it may not be as easy as we think), God has promised that the plans that He has for us will be for a good future ahead. He knows the plans that He has set out to for us, even when we are overwhelmed by the calamity around us.

> *"I know the plans I have for you,"* declares the Lord, *"plans to prosper you and not to harm you, plans to give you hope and a future."*
> **(Jeremiah 29:11)**

As we become confident that He will begin a good work in us, the hope which is in God will fill us with joy and peace as we put our trust in Him. We may have a handful of plans that we would like to accomplish, but God's purpose succeeds abundantly.

Write down your vision for the future; what will take you to the next level?

~ CHAPTER THIRTEEN ~

Women of Unshakeable Faith

BE THE BEST YOU

"It is not what we get. But who we become, what gives meaning to our lives"

~ Tony Robbins ~

The power of God will be behind every decision you make in this new season of your life. Why on earth did we have to go through the long and lengthy process to get to where we are now?

I sincerely believe that wisdom comes with age. Most definitely! If you had dreamt about what was in your future, would you have done something much better? I honestly think we would if we had known what we now know. Sometimes God's plan for our lives may not be one that we fully understand, but I know that everything we perceive as evil He will work for our good!!

'Let go and live' is one of my themes this year, which has enabled me to forgive and let go of past hurts. The only reason I had been holding on to them was that I did not know how to let go and be free from them.

Forgiving someone who has wronged me in the past, and forgiving my past failures and woes, has helped me to mature with strength. As we go through the motion of life and trivial things that upsets us, we can stand firm knowing that God, our Redeemer, sits on the Throne.

Standing as women of God with unshakeable faith brings hope that is not limited to our human expectations. We can move forward and do the things that God has called us to, without the guilt laid on us by others.

Emotions can leave us torn and battered where life has not treated us well. We can be afraid of losing our loved ones because the old issues have made their way into our relationships, our marriages and even in our Churches. But as we hold on to faith, unshakeable faith, we will see mountains move, doors opening and many opportunities knocking on the door.

Faith merely believes in something we are hoping to receive.

The Word of God says Faith is:
> *"...the substance of things hoped for,*
> *the evidence of things not seen"*
> **(Hebrews 11:1 NKJV)**

Women of unshakeable faith who have determination, perseverance and hope never doubt that their victories will come, and when they do, they are never doubtful of where they came from. It is the Well from which springs the waters of answered prayers, fervent and persevering prayers. As women, naturally, we dream about and hope for many things for now and the future, for ourselves and our families. We sometimes dream about a new house, less financial debt so we can enjoy the life that God has given us, a different job; the list is endless.

Women of unshakeable faith who **persevere** will continue to hold out, no matter how the winds will blow, sometimes even for years, to see their faith strengthen. For the women of unshakeable faith, there may be things that we hope for, that involve more profound matters of the heart. Perhaps that woman of God is praying for a loved one to have a relationship with God, or maybe she has been waiting for the right husband. Fervently she may pray to God to change the circumstance that she has no control over. But one thing is sure, all of these things require the **virtue of faith**.

Hannah's faith to trust God and her determination to have a son was her belief that He would give her a son; she never gave up on hope. Her commitment to continue praying gave her **hope** that God would answer her prayer. Although she was seemingly barren, God delayed her bringing forth a child, because He had a plan! Her faith in God was so sincere that she promised that she would give back her son to the service of God. *"...when the time had come about after Hannah had conceived, that she bare a son and called his name Samuel, saying because I have asked him of the Lord."* (I Samuel 1:20) *"...then I will bring him, that he may appear before the Lord, and there abide forever."* (I Samuel 1:22)

Another woman of unshakeable faith was **Mary** who historically gave birth to the Son of Man. She had faith that God was going to fulfil His promise and bring forth the Messiah through her, even though she was an unwed virgin. God's plan was carried out through the birth, death and the resurrection of Jesus Christ.

Anna, the Prophetess, whose faith was unshakeable through the loss of her husband of seven years, saw her faith that stood the test of time. At the age of eighty-four, she fasted and prayed while she persevered against the odds of being a widow at an early age. She never left the Temple where she lived, praying and fasting night and day. Because of her fervent prayers she was honoured to see the Messiah coming into the Temple as a baby. (Luke 2:36-38).

Esther's faith was unshakeable as she remained faithful to her people. She risked losing everything, even her life, when she confronted her husband, the King, to save her people from the hands of Haman.

"If I perish I perish!" were the last words she told her people. Her unshakeable faith found favour with the King.

> *"...Esther put on her royal robes and stood in the inner court of the palace, in front of the king's hall. The king was sitting on his royal throne in the hall, facing the entrance. When he saw Queen Esther standing in the court, he was pleased with her and held out to her the gold sceptre that was in his hand. So, Esther approached and touched the tip of the sceptre."*
> **(Esther 5:1-2)**

Ruth, another woman with unshakeable faith, and an honourable and a virtuous woman who believed in Naomi's God. *"Your people will be my people and your God will be my God. Where you lodge I will lodge,"* Ruth said to Naomi. She followed Naomi back to her hometown, but because she believed in the God that Naomi served and was faithful to Naomi, she obtained the unshakeable faith through her perseverance in the field, where she met her Boaz. (Ruth 1:14-22)

Dorcas with unshakeable faith when she cared for other widows who had lost their husbands. She continued to show compassion to those who were sorrowful and did not put her feelings above anyone else's. The Bible states in Acts 9:36 that she was 'rich in the acts of kindness and charity.' Similar to Anna, she showed compassion to those who were in crisis after losing their husband. Broken women who were experiencing grief longed for comfort from other bereaved women. But, because of Dorcas's unshakeable faith, God saw her work and when she died suddenly, she was raised from death to care for the women she continued to show compassion.

Deborah, an ordinary housewife, a Prophetess and a spokeswoman for God, had guided her to victory. She was a woman with unshakeable faith. She stood firm against all the odds of the Israelites in Judges 4:4-10. She had remarkable confidence and she trusted in God to take her through dangerous situations she was not in control.

There are many examples of women in the Bible who held fast to their faith regardless of the visible circumstances and obstacles. Faith takes patience, things hoped for; it does not always come immediately. For the woman of unshakeable faith, it helps for her to trust in a God who knows her every desire before she even speaks it. But most importantly, she recognises the promises of God's Word.

The faith of a Christian woman is dependent on her belief in God. Even in her darkest hour, she can stand, knowing that God will fulfil His promises in her life. God promises strength for the faint of heart, mercy for the weak, forgiveness for the repentant, protection for the vulnerable. Because God is faithful, every Christian woman who has unshakeable faith can rest knowing that she has put her faith in a God who will never disappoint her.

Unshakeable faith is what drives the heart to not quit, even when the circumstances look bleak. Something within a woman of faith says she is not going anywhere until God comes through for her! She will not be moved by her circumstances, and it does not matter how she feels, nor how many times the situation looks bleak from the outside. Faith is what plants the feet of the woman of unshakeable faith firmly on the promises of God.

I pray as you go through this book that you begin to realise that God loves you and He wants the best for you. As you stand firm and be the woman or man of faith, God will reward you in abundance.

God is looking for women that will stand and be bold in their situation. The women that 'moves the hand' of God will be prayer warriors who dedicate her life to service. When facing danger, they will be active on the battlefield when real courage through genuine modesty is in numbers.

Write down the things that would allow you to be a woman of unshakeable faith:

_____
_____
_____
_____
_____
_____
_____
_____
_____
_____
_____
_____
_____
_____

Conclusion

"Only those who have learned the power of sincere and selfless contribution experience life's deepest joy: true fulfilment."
~ **Tony Robbins** ~

If you want more clarity in the knowledge that God can do the impossible, I am convinced reading this book will help you understand how He is working in your situation. If you have, at this point, and you are allowing the Holy Spirit to minister to you, you are half-way there.

There are steps that you may have to take to turn your issues of rejection and self-blame around. The first step towards your healing is to **identify the problem** you are facing and the root cause. So often we do not call the problem by its name; **Rejection, Abandonment, Soul Ties, and Unforgiveness**.

Secondly, **accept** that God will help you to overcome those obstacles, and for many of us, there are multiple of issues that we cannot release from and **begin a life of peace and joy**. But when you forgive and move on it will help you get to the next level in your new season, adhering to the Word of God. Also, these things will accomplish when you change your situation and not allowing unforgiveness to be a part of your destiny.

Although you cannot change what has happened to you, nor go back to the past, you can forget the past or see it from a different perspective, one that shows us how God has worked it out for your good. God will open doors that were closed and shut some doors in our life. You will **receive your victory** and be free from the obstacles that have prevented you from moving forward. Your victory is coming!

You have read my story, and you have seen what God has done in my life. Now you can allow God to reshape your life and 'rid' the obstacles that prevent you from taking the leap of faith. Nothing in this world is impossible for God. When you entrust God with your life, He will give you the freedom of peace and joy. Your victory begins today when you release every hurt and self-doubt to God. I am free and not bound by my past any longer. Today you will **claim what is yours!**

It is a beautiful feeling to have the love from people that mean so much to us. We all want to be loved because we were all created by God's love. For many who struggle with the pain of rejection and self-hate, the journey seems as though it will never end. It may have been overwhelming and full of surprises that we cannot believe that we have invited in some of the hurt we may now or have experienced.

Moving on from past hurts, the wounded hearts and brokenness that have scarred our lives is where our new journey begins. Together we will get through this, and you have taken steps to **move forward and leave the past behind**. It is time to let go and receive what God has promised to you.

Receive the promise today with these declarations:
"Today, I decree and declare that **He will give you strength** when you are tired, and He will increase the power of the weak." (Isaiah 40:29)

"I declare that those who hope in the Lord will **renew their strength**. They will soar on wings like eagles; they will run and not grow weary, they will walk and not be faint." (Isaiah 40:31)

"Today, **I will not fear** because God is with me. I will not be alarmed or dismayed for He is God. He will strengthen me and help me; He will uphold me with His righteous right hand." (Isaiah 41:10)

"I decree that the Lord your God who takes hold of your right hand and says to you, **do not fear**; will help you." (Isaiah 41:13)

"When you pass through the waters, **He will be with you**; and when you pass through the rivers, they will not sweep over you. When you walk through the fire, you will not be burned; the flames will not set you ablaze." (Isaiah 43:2)

What if things were different?

Have you ever considered what it would be like if the things that have happened to you never occurred in the first place? Believe it or not, you would not be the person that you have become if that were so. Sometimes God allows obstacles to come in your way to propel you to greatness and be the best that you are!

Did you know that you are only as strong as your greatest fear? Your weakest link? Your strength will show up greatly as your fears show up. **Be courageous** while God directs you to the destiny that you are assigned to have, and allow Him to make you the best you can be; your best self as He wants you to be.

The first sign of maturity comes from a heart of obedience; trusting God with your decisions and your life. **Be free from the opinions of others**; their opinions are the very reason that held you in the past in the first place! At times, life will get you down; I know this too well. But always know that you can **achieve the impossible** if you fix your eyes on God. Some storms may come to help us to grow and propel us to soar like an eagle. God desires us to be just that; an eagle.

You have to accept that some storms, will come in order for us to grow and learn, but God's love remains unconditional, and He is faithful to us when we allow Him to be in everything that we do. It is easy for us to comfortably put God in a box, and dust Him off when and how we need Him. But God is not limited to our circumstances nor our failures. Because of His grace and mercy which is sufficient for us, we can be overcomers and victorious.

Time is a healer, and it has been both a process and a challenge for me. There was never a time did I think for one moment that God was preparing me for my healing and for writing a book!

For you to overcome the dark areas of your life, it has to begin with a process. A process to help you to mature and take risk; moving towards something much bigger than yourself and overcome the fear to **change your situation**. You have to **take up the challenge** to overcome those challenges that keep you locked in a box.

People may not notice or appreciate the difference in you nor may they comprehend the changes that are taking place as God prepares you for what may be impossible to see. However, many of those around you, whose eyes are dim spiritually, can only remember who you were before you let go of your past. Instead of seeing you as a new person they continue to hold on to the 'past' you.

But if you focus on the positive aspects of your attributes, you will find your footing in the things you never dreamed or imagined yourself doing. Opportunities will open doors to new favours, as you step into your God-given destiny. The change begins with you before you can see others through spiritual eyes.

The journey was set up for our correction. Although it may have been painful to listen or hear God, He was setting the process to work through our pain and brokenness. Sometimes brokenness may come because we have compromised wisdom and therefore failed to gain understanding through the Word. By putting our trust and hope in Jesus Christ, we can overcome and conquer fear.

As we remain obedient and listen to the instruction of the Holy Spirit, God will steer us, like a navigator, to our divine calling, our vision and our destiny! The hope that will get you into the presence of God as you continue to be obedient will help you remember to rely on Him to get you to the place where you ought to be.

> *"Behold, I show you a mystery; We shall not all sleep, but we shall all be changed, in a moment, in the twinkling of an eye…"*
> **(Corinthians 15:51)**

I am encouraging you to take that step of boldness today and forgive those who have hurt you. Although my parents may not have made the right decisions, forgiving them was the only way forward. But most importantly, they are also human and subject to the same mistakes and failures as anyone else. Also, if you are a reader who is struggling with life's issues, forgiveness is the only real-life factor that will release you from the burden of unforgiveness. Take up the challenge today and forgive not only yourself but others.

Let go and live!

> *"As you begin to master the art of letting go, with patience, dedication and love, your reality will change. It has no choice. In the process of letting go, you will lose many things from the past, but you will find yourself. It will be a permanent Self, rooted in awareness…."*
>
> **~ Deepak Chopra ~**

You may be reading this book and wondering, 'how can it be!' But the Word of God teaches us to be humble and trust Him with all that is going on in our lives.

> *"Come to me, who labour and are heavy laden, and I will give you rest, take my yoke upon you, and I will give you rest!"*
> **(Matthew 11:30)**

The Word of God declares in Psalm 126:5-6 *"they that sow in tears shall reap in joy. But those that weep carrying precious seeds will return rejoicing in joy"*.

This is one of the many things we get with the revelation of God's love. It can be an overwhelming experience but joyful. His love is the fundamental cornerstone upon which our faith stands. The love that He gives us enables us to step out in faith without the fear factor.

If you are feeling overwhelmed, I encourage you that His love for you will conquer all fear and His word will convince you of His love.

By the renewing of your mind, you will be changed inside and out for God's purpose. We must not comply with our efforts by the expectation and demands of others but be transformed into what is right and acceptable to God.

Finding joy through pain is the by-product of this experience, and it is incredible when you exchange sorrow and sadness to joy. It is a feeling of contentment and achievement that comes few and far between.

About the Author

Monica Ambersley was born in London, England.

She is a Certified Life Coach and a Christian blogger who writes and passionately aims to encourage, inspire and motivate women. Her desire is to coach women, especially young women, to step into their destiny.

She has a Diploma in Biblical Theology and is currently studying for a Bachelor Degree in Ministry. She also has a Bachelor Degree in Finance and Management and is presently working within finance.

She has worked with young people for over fourteen years as a Youth President and has seen them grow into beautiful men and women.

Since writing her first book, *From Pain to Joy*, she is now on the right path to excel where God has planned and worked it out for her. Her healing process throughout her life has been an incredible journey, and it has taken her to another level as she decreed and declared the Word over her life and the life of her children and every young person.

While applying the love of God and motivating others to push until they see something happen, God has opened doors to new opportunities.

In 2016, she started her online Ministry, *Abundance of Faith*, locally and internationally through various social media, Periscope and Facebook Live. She continues to share and encourage the Word of God to many on social media as a Speaker.

You can contact her for speaking engagements via email:
Abundanceoffaith@hotmail.com

or visit her website: **http://wwww.Abundanceoffaith.com**
where you will be motivated and encouraged.

To contact author:
Facebook: @MonicaAmbersleyAuthor
Periscope: @Monicaa_Amb
Instagram: @Monicaa_Amb

References

1. Steven R. Asher, et al, Peer Rejection in Childhood, Cambridge University Press, USA, 1990, p. 253

2. https://www.childrenssociety.org.uk

3. Website: Amelia Hill, theguardian.com, How the UK halved its teenage pregnancy rate, 18th July 2016

4. Monroe, Dr Myles, 7 Principles of an Eagle

5. Blakes, R.C, Jr, The Father Daughter Talk, Life Bridge Books, Charlotte, NC, 2014, p. 98

6. The Bible, New International Version – Psalm 27:4

www.ingramcontent.com/pod-product-compliance
Lightning Source LLC
Chambersburg PA
CBHW070953080526
44587CB00015B/2289